Professional Development Series:
Interactive Module Workbook

Curriculum Technology, LLC

Contributors:
Jennifer Arzberger
Brooke McAuley
Cyndi McNeal
Randall Myers
Kimberly Souza

Developmental Editors:
Kristin Brabec
Maggie DeAngelis

Curriculum Technology, LLC
Oceanside, CA

Professional Development Series: Interactive Module Workbook
Copyright 2013 by Curriculum Technology, LLC.
All Rights Reserved.

Printed in the United States of America

No part of this publication may be reproduced, stored in a retrieval system, or transmitted in any form or by any means electronic, mechanical, photocopying, recording, or otherwise without prior written permission of both the publisher and the copyright holder of this book.

Photo editor: Karen Allen and the public domain.

Publisher: Channel Custom, 3520 Seagate Way, Suite 115, Oceanside, CA 92056.

Manufactured in the United States of America, 1st edition,
Curriculum Technology, LLC, 2013.

Professional Development Series: Interactive Module Workbook. A workbook by
Curriculum Technology, LLC. Oceanside, California. 1st edition, 2013.

ISBN 978-1-938087-04-2

WARNING: Re-creation of any case study or event listed in the materials may result in injury or property damage if extensive care is not taken at all times. Curriculum Technology and Channel Publishing are not responsible for any injuries or damage to property that may occur from the use of referenced equipment or any other supplies.

Experiments and activities derived from this book should be conducted with oversight by, and at the direction of, a qualified instructor.
***
This textbook contains completely original content unless otherwise specified. Due diligence was taken in the evaluation of this content to protect the copyrights of others. Any duplication of any copyrighted material or any content found within this textbook that is improperly cited is completely unintentional.

Professional Development Series:
Interactive Module Workbook

Supplement to the Professional Development iMods

Table of Contents

Preface	**6**
Module 1: Motivation and Attitude	**7**
Lesson	8
Independent Practice 1	19
Independent Practice 2	20
Group Activity	21
Knowledge Check	22
Module 2: Group Dynamics	**25**
Lesson	26
Independent Practice 1	37
Independent Practice 2	38
Group Activity	39
Knowledge Check	40
Module 3: Conflict Resolution	**43**
Lesson	44
Independent Practice 1	55
Independent Practice 2	56
Group Activity	57
Knowledge Check	58
Module 4: Workplace Behaviors	**61**
Lesson	62
Independent Practice 1	73
Independent Practice 2	74
Group Activity	75
Knowledge Check	76
Module 5: Job Search Skills	**79**
Lesson	80
Independent Practice 1	95
Independent Practice 2	96
Group Activity	97
Knowledge Check	98

Table of Contents cont.

Module 6: Interview Preparation — **101**
Lesson — 102
Independent Practice 1 — 113
Independent Practice 2 — 115
Group Activity — 116
Knowledge Check — 117

Module 7: Customer Service — **119**
Lesson — 120
Independent Practice 1 — 130
Independent Practice 2 — 131
Group Activity — 133
Knowledge Check — 134

Module 8: Career Planning — **137**
Lesson — 138
Independent Practice 1 — 148
Independent Practice 2 — 149
Group Activity — 150
Knowledge Check — 151

Module 9: Business Basics — **153**
Lesson — 154
Independent Practice 1 — 166
Independent Practice 2 — 167
Group Activity — 167
Knowledge Check — 168

Module 10: Externship Excellence — **171**
Lesson — 172
Independent Practice 1 — 182
Independent Practice 2 — 183
Group Activity — 184
Knowledge Check — 185

About the Contributors

Jennifer Arzberger, Ph.D. ABD
Having spent a number of years as an Instructional Coach for Littleton Public Schools in Colorado, Jennifer currently holds the position of Executive Director for a new charter school opening in Colorado. Jennifer is a Ph.D. candidate in Curriculum and Instruction.

Brooke McAuley, MSW, CACIII
Currently a counselor and life coach for her own private practice in Denver, Colorado, Brooke has primarily worked in the addiction research and treatment field. Brooke has a Masters in Social Work and is a Certified Addictions Counselor III.

Cyndi McNeal
As a Licensed Vocational Nurse, Cyndi has worked in various nursing related positions. She received her teaching credential from University of California, Riverside, and has a vast amount of experience in the healthcare field.

Randall Myers, MBA
Currently an Associate Dean at Stevens-Henager College, Randy is a retired US Navy Captain. Randy's background is in Finance, and he is the creator of Bloomerizing the Curriculum, a model for designing curriculum.

Kimberly Souza, MA
Kimberly has worked as an Adjunct Professor at DeVry University and Kaplan University. In addition, she has teamed with NASA as an educational programs manager. Kimberly has a Masters in Curriculum and Instruction Computer Education.

Preface

About this Workbook

The Professional Development Series: iMod Workbook has been designed as a companion workbook for Curriculum Technology's Professional Development Interactive Modules (iMods). iMods, a powerful tool for teaching focused instructional units, provide instructors and students with an opportunity to explore important skills used every day by professionals in the workplace. Meant to supplement academic theory learned in the classroom, iMods provide a connection between key concepts, hands on learning, skill based instruction and practical application.

Promising to increase engagement and understanding, this workbook is comprised of eleven professional development modules. Developed to be used in conjunction with the iMod series, this workbook can also stand alone as a classroom resource for teaching Professional Development to students. Through the integration of content, practice exercises, discussions, and assignments, the workbook facilitates opportunities for valuable collaboration. Explicitly identifying strategies that support cooperative learning, you'll discover that this resource helps to increase professionalism as well as students' beliefs in their own ability to achieve.

Module 1

Motivation and Attitude

Objectives:

– **Understand how motivation improves productivity in the workplace**

– **Identify the outcomes of a good attitude**

– **Define self-efficacy**

Motivation and Attitude

Maintaining a positive attitude will prepare you for success.

Self-efficacy is critical to your personal and professional achievement.

There are a number of ways to prepare for success. Maintaining a positive attitude about your skills and abilities is a major factor. In this module, you will learn about self-efficacy, which is critical to your personal and professional achievement. Learning what factors and actions are important in building a strong sense of self-efficacy can lead to greater academic, professional, and personal success. As you work through this module, think of other ways you can reinforce this information.

What Do You Already Know?

Directions: Place a check mark next to the factors that affect your motivation in the workplace and in your personal life.

Past experiences	
The potential for promotions and pay raises	
Your personal hopes, dreams, and goals	
Your overall attitude toward life	
The opinions of your employer and colleagues, or other people you respect	

Motivation as a Driving Force

Motivation helps us to achieve our goals. It is why we act in a certain way and why we want particular things. It pushes us in a direction to accomplish objectives. It is what provokes us to take action. Motivation is a force that can change your attitude, strengthen your actions, and increase your **productivity**.

There are two types of motivation:

>**External (extrinsic) motivation:** External motivators are outside of the actual work itself, such as a promised reward or recognition.

>**Internal (intrinsic) motivation:** The stronger of the two types of motivation, internal motivation is an intense driving force that comes from the underlying value of the work.

Internal and external motivations are very important to everything we do. They are an essential part of our productivity and accomplishments.

> Productivity: The efficient and effective use of resources, with minimum waste and effort to achieve an outcome

> Internal (intrinsic) motivation: Comes from the desire to be something, to obtain something, or to have something

> External (extrinsic) motivation: Comes from external forces and people that are causing you to do something

Motivation and Productivity

People are motivated by a variety of factors:

Motivation and productivity are what employers seek.

> Providing for a family
> Enjoying their work
> Making a name in their field
> Gaining experience

Motivated people have increased productivity. Being productive helps you feel successful and happy in the work that you do.

Employers seek individuals who are motivated and productive. Individuals who are enthusiastic about their job are often very reliable. Such people will do whatever it takes to reach the goals of the organization. Their pride shines through in their work. Less motivated workers don't put in as much effort. That extra effort is what boosts productivity and is ultimately what employers are looking for in an employee.

 Discussion Question

What motivates you to succeed?

Practice

Directions: Read each task and decide if it is internal motivation or external motivation.

Task	Internal Motivation or External Motivation
You read a non-fiction book because you are curious about the topic.	
You attend all of your classes this semester so you can learn as much as possible.	
You plan to achieve good grades so your parents will buy you a car.	
You select a major in college based on the latest salary statistics.	
You stay up late working on an assignment to make sure it is done correctly because it makes you feel good to submit your best work.	
You stay late to finish a project so you can be paid time and a half.	

What Does Attitude Have to Do with Success?

Attitude:

> Optimist: A person who sees the best in situations; someone who is hopeful

> Pessimist: A person who expects the worst outcome in any given situation

> Determines how you think, feel, and act
> Influences your view of a person, thing, or situation

Someone with a positive attitude is an optimist. A person with a negative attitude is considered a pessimist. A pessimist always thinks the glass is "half empty." An optimist deals with challenging events in positive and productive ways.

"A positive mental attitude is the starting point of all riches, whether they be riches of a material nature or intangible riches."

– Napoleon Hill

Discussion Questions

> Can you think of someone in your life who is an optimist?
>
> How do they deal with challenges?
>
> How can you be more of an optimist?

Choose Your Attitude

Your attitude is a personal choice. It's important to understand the differences between a positive and negative attitude, since your thoughts will shape your reality and future.

A Person with a Positive Attitude	A Person with a Negative Attitude
Finds the "hidden gift" in a negative situation	Finds negativity in most situations
Anticipates happiness and successful outcomes	Always finds something to worry about
Copes more easily with difficult situations	Feels nothing is ever quite right
Believes defeat is only temporary	Feels that bad events last forever
Lives a more fulfilled life	Lives in fear and sadness

Cultivate a Positive Attitude

How can you develop a positive attitude?

> Make sure your thoughts are uplifting and positive
> Think about and appreciate the positive aspects of your life
> Be accountable for your actions and their consequences
> Surround yourself with positive and supportive people

The benefits of a positive attitude include:

> Greater levels of happiness and inner strength
> More energy
> Inspiration and motivation for yourself and others
> Additional motivation to achieve goals and success

Discussion Questions

Who are some positive people you know?

What about their outlook strikes you as exceptional?

What is it about their attitudes that you would like to cultivate for yourself?

 Practice

Directions: Read the following list of outcomes. Decide if they are an outcome of a positive attitude or NOT an outcome of a positive attitude. Write each in the correct category below.

> Better outlook on life and situations
> Feeling overwhelming stress
> Upbeat and pleasant to be around
> Feeling in control of your life
> Expecting the worst to happen
> Having more energy

Outcome of a Positive Attitude	NOT an Outcome of a Positive Attitude

Assignment

Achievement Journal

Developing and maintaining a positive attitude is something you can practice every day. Repeat affirmations, which are positive statements about yourself, to practice a positive attitude.

Directions: In the space provided below, write out five positive statements and refer to them throughout the day. Some examples include:

"Today will be a great day."
"I feel great! I am full of energy and able to accomplish anything today."
"I can do anything I set my mind to."

Affirmations

1.

2.

3.

4.

5.

Set the tone of the day by reviewing these affirmations in the morning and reciting them throughout the day.

Self-esteem: A favorable opinion of oneself

Self-concept: A set of opinions and attitudes that one has of oneself

What is Self-Efficacy?

Motivation and a positive attitude will help you develop strong sense of self-efficacy. Self-efficacy is the belief in your ability to achieve a goal. If you believe you can complete a particular job, you have a high sense of self-efficacy. If you do not believe you are able to do something, your sense of self-efficacy is weak.

Self-efficacy differs from self-esteem or self-concept, which are based on how we feel about ourselves. Self-efficacy focuses on whether we believe we can accomplish a specific task. It plays a major role in how we respond to situations. It influences the choices we make, how hard we work at a task, how we deal with obstacles, or how quickly we give up when the job gets tough.

"People with high assurance in their capabilities approach difficult tasks as challenges to be mastered rather than as threats to be avoided." – *Alfred Bandura*

Strong vs. Weak Self-Efficacy

Individuals with a strong sense of self-efficacy:

> View challenges as tasks to be mastered
> Develop deeper interest in, and commitment to, activities
> Recover quickly from setbacks and disappointment

Individuals with a weak sense of self-efficacy:

> Do not expect to do well
> Avoid challenging tasks because they think they will fail
> Focus on personal failings and negative outcomes
> Give up before even starting
> Usually do not achieve at their ability level

Four Factors that Contribute to a Strong Sense of Self-Efficacy

The four major factors that contribute to a strong sense of self-efficacy are: observing others, past performances, positive feedback, and a winning attitude.

Observing Others	When you see other people successfully complete a task, it strengthens your belief in your own ability to complete that same job. Make a point to observe others completing a similar task successfully.
Past Performances	Your performance on a similar project is the greatest influence on your current sense of self-efficacy. If you were successful in the past, your sense of self-efficacy will be strong. However, a poorly performed task will weaken your sense of self-efficacy. For poorly performed tasks, you will need to reflect and think of ways to strengthen that skill. Practice makes perfect.
Positive Feedback	When someone we respect believes in us, our self-efficacy increases. A simple " You can do it!" from a person who matters to you can have a huge impact on your success. Embrace all the positive feedback you receive.
Winning Attitude	Emotions are related to self-efficacy. A positive view can boost your spirits, while anxiety or fear can threaten your sense of self-efficacy. Practice a positive attitude every day.

Practice

Directions: Place a check mark next to the characteristics displayed by a person with a strong sense of self-efficacy.

View challenges as tasks to be mastered	
Believe difficult tasks are beyond their capabilities	
Develop a deep interest in activities they participate in	
Give up before ever starting	
Work hard and persist in the face of adversity	
Believe they can accomplish the task	

Assignment

Directions: Journaling is a great tool to learn more about yourself. Use the space below to write down a challenging situation you've faced and defeated. Explain what did you do to overcome this obstacle, and what it showed you.

_____

_____

_____

_____

_____

_____

_____

Independent Practice 1

Directions: Read the following scenario of a student and teacher in a classroom. Think about the four major factors that contribute to a strong sense of self-efficacy. Answer the questions when you are finished.

Teacher: *Thanks for staying after class to talk with me, Ben.*

Student: *Yeah, no problem.*

Teacher: *I wanted to talk to you about something I overheard during class. I heard you telling your partner that you didn't care and weren't going to complete the assigned activities.*

Student: *Yeah, it's just that I don't understand the topic and I don't like it at all. No matter what, I'm not going to do it right anyway.*

Teacher: *Well, Ben, you need to believe in yourself and give it a try. I know you can do it, and I will be here for extra support. I suggest you come into class early tomorrow and I can be here to answer any questions.*

Student: *Okay, I guess that'll work. See you tomorrow.*

Teacher: *Great, Ben. Have a good rest of your day.*

Answer Bank
past performances
weak
social persuasion

1. The student in this scenario displays a _____ sense of self-efficacy.

2. Ben did not think he would do well because of _____.

3. In order to help Ben with his sense of self-efficacy, the teacher used _____.

Independent Practice 2

Directions: Read each example and use the answer bank to complete the sentences.

Answer Bank
motivation
self-efficacy
attitude

Example 1
Students are entering a classroom and getting ready to take a midterm. One student sits calmly because she knows that she generally does well on exams and she feels certain that she will do well on this one. Another student is distressed because he did not do well on the last exam, and he is fearful of failing again.

1. This is an example of _____.

Example 2
Student 1: *Carlos wakes up on time with a positive attitude, gets ready for class, has all of his class supplies organized, and is ready for the exam.*

Student 2: *Mario wakes up late, evidence of a late night. His class supplies are disorganized, and he is dropping things on the way to his car. He runs into class late for the exam and does not have a pencil.*

2. This is an example of _____.

Example 3
A class is given an assignment. Grumbling comes from the class, but a particular student is thinking about the upcoming assignment, what it will take to get the best grade, and the steps needed to complete the work. The student is focused on getting good grades and finishing the assignment; the student is breaking the assignment down into manageable pieces and visualizing the final result.

3. This is an example of _____.

 **Group Activity**

Having a positive attitude is very important to your academic and professional success.

Directions: Complete the following tasks.

1. List 5 or 6 behaviors of someone with a positive attitude.

_____   _____

_____   _____

_____   _____

2. Within your group, you will be acting out a job interview.
Select three people in your group to play the following roles:

> Interviewer
> Applicant with positive attitude
> Applicant with negative attitude

The interviewer will ask the following:

> Tell me about your previous experience.
> Why do you want to work for this company?
> Are you a team player?

Reflection: After the role-play, reflect on the following questions individually.

> Which candidate would you hire and why?
> Which candidate displayed a positive attitude?
> Which candidate displayed a negative attitude?

_____

_____

_____

_____

_____

Knowledge Check

Directions: Circle the correct answer.

1. What is NOT one of the four major influences on a strong sense of self-efficacy?

a) Past performances

b) Observing others

c) Peer pressure

d) Positive feedback

2. External motivation comes from

a.) How we feel about ourselves

b.) A promised reward or recognition

c.) The work itself

d.) A cause we feel strongly about

3. Internal motivation is _____ external motivation.

a.) Weaker than

b.) Similar to

c.) The same as

d.) Stronger than

4. Self-efficacy _____ how we feel about ourselves.

a.) Is directly related to

b.) Is not related to

c.) Has no impact on

d.) Has little impact on

5. Our past performance on a similar task

a.) Does not contribute toward our sense of self-efficacy

b.) Enhances our self-esteem but does not affect our sense of self-efficacy

c.) Is the greatest contribution to our sense of self-efficacy

d.) Does not enhance our self-esteem nor contribute to our sense of self-efficacy

6. A poor performance on a similar task

a.) Will enhance our sense of self-efficacy

b.) Will weaken our sense of self-efficacy

c.) Does not impact our sense of self-efficacy

d.) All of the above

7. Having a positive attitude can

a.) Affect your life

b.) Affect your expectations

c.) Affect your behaviors

d.) All of the above

8. Motivation is defined as

a.) Our desire for money

b.) Something everyone has

c.) A driving force that pushes us to achieve our goals

d.) None of the above

9. A positive attitude can have an impact on

a.) Your relationships with others

b.) The material things in your life

c.) Your outlook on life

d.) Both a and c

10. Our sense of self-efficacy plays an important role in:

a.) How successful we are

b.) How long we persist in the face of challenges

c.) How we view situations

d.) All of these above

Group Dynamics

Objectives:

– Identify appropriate communication styles, behaviors and boundaries when working with a supervisor, a coworker or a subordinate

– Understand the elements of effective teamwork in group and workplace settings

Group Dynamics

You play a vital role in your team.

It is crucial to understand group dynamics.

As you prepare for success in the workplace, it is crucial to understand group dynamics. As a member of the workforce, you play a vital role in your team. It is important to know how to effectively interact with the various members of your organization both individually and in a group setting. In this module, you will learn how to communicate with others while considering workplace roles and relationships. These skills will help you become an invaluable member of your organization.

What Do You Already Know?

Directions: Think about a time when you worked in an academic or professional group setting. Decide if the following statements are true or false.

Statement	True	False
It's inappropriate to discuss personal problems when working in a group		
Non-verbal cues, like body language, can show a lot about how a person is feeling		
Effective communication is important when working in a group		
Groups go through different stages of development		
An effective leader leads by example		

Success in Groups

Working in teams can be one of the best approaches to producing high quality work in a professional setting. Through collaboration, a group can accomplish more in a shorter period of time. In addition, the products and solutions developed through teamwork are often better, as a result of the diverse background, experience, and knowledge of team members.

Generally speaking, teams in a work setting consist of colleagues whom you work with on a daily basis. These individuals are categorized into one of the three groups:

> Coworkers
> Supervisors
> **Subordinates**

Sometimes your team may include other participants like:

> **Clients**
> Patients
> **Vendors**

Having the ability to work well in a team will greatly impact the success of your career. You can learn to be an effective team member by recognizing appropriate and effective interactions, valuing various perspectives, and learning what to do during the stages of group development.

Subordinates: Someone lower in rank or position

Clients: Those who pay for the products and services your business provides

Vendors: Those who provides products or services to your business

Valuing Perspective

When working in a team, it is important to remember that each individual has their own thoughts and ideas about how to approach a task. Every person has a different background and experience, creating a unique point of view. This is often referred to as someone's **perspective**.

When interacting with others, keep perspective in mind. Like the old saying, "two heads are better than one," be open to other people's thoughts and how they **perceive** situations. Remember that you're all working towards the same goal. Keeping perspective in mind will help you to develop a stronger and more well rounded team.

Perspective: A personal outlook

Perceive: What someone thinks of an idea

Discussion Question

How can I try to remain open-minded while working in a team?

Practice

Directions: View the figure below. Count how many rectangles you see and write down your answer.

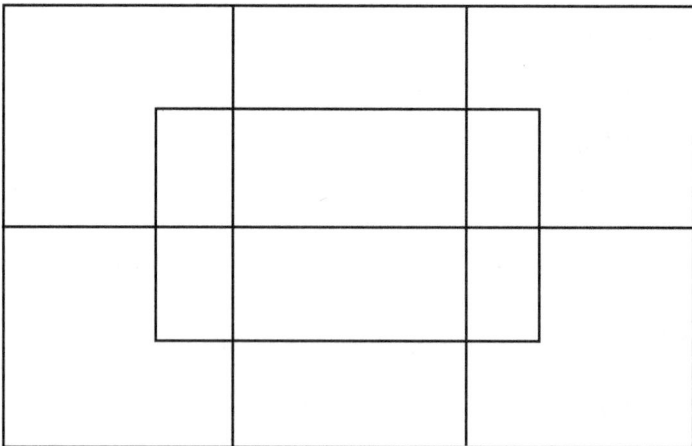

Number of rectangles: _____.

In this exercise, it is likely for the number of rectangles to differ. Some people overlook rectangles, while others search for ways to create more rectangles. People perceive things differently. Be aware of perceptions and opinions of others while working in a group.

 **Assignment**

Directions: Using complete sentences, answer the following questions below.

1. Looking at the rectangle image, why do you think answers differ between people?

2. What does this activity teach us about varying perspectives?

_____
_____
_____
_____
_____
_____
_____
_____
_____
_____
_____

Interacting with Your Supervisor

Your supervisor is an integral part of your career development. Your supervisor helps you establish benchmarks for success, interprets your actions, and offers the resources you need to be successful. It is important that your interactions with your supervisor remain professional.

Tips for successful interactions with your supervisor:

> Be clear and concise when communicating

> Be prepared

> Always show respect

> Openly accept responsibilities

> Present yourself confidently

> Stay positive

> Keep conversations appropriate

Build a productive working relationship.

Focus on building a productive working relationship with your supervisor. Building this relationship will greatly help you be successful in your career.

"Your relationship with your new boss will be built through a series of conversations."

– *Michael Watkins*

 **Practice**

Directions: Read each type of conversation. Choose if each conversation is appropriate or inappropriate to have with your supervisor. Draw a happy face in the box for appropriate conversations and a sad face for inappropriate conversations.

Gain knowledge of your supervisor's role, professional background, and vision	
Ask questions that deepen your knowledge of the organization's mission and goals	
Discuss personal issues and drama with family, relationships and coworkers	
Clarify your role, job expectations, and execution of job tasks	
Verbalize complaints that lack solution	
Ask questions that can be answered through your own initiative	

Interacting with Coworkers and Peers

Interactions with your coworkers may be less formal than interactions with your boss. You will develop **camaraderie** among your coworkers as you continue to work together. Friendships in the workplace can foster an enjoyable work environment.

Camaraderie: Friendship

Although it's favorable to have friendships in the workplace, it's important to remain professional. A great way to maintain a professional behavior and still have friendships is to demonstrate leadership traits. Try to set an example and think of yourself as a leader.

> Develop a good awareness of your personal and professional boundaries

> Focus on your work while at work

> Stay away from gossip

> Do your part in working toward common goals

> Show gratitude

> Show an interest and listen to others

TIP: *Plan ahead. Think of a few things you can say next time a coworker wants to gossip with you.*

 Assignment

Directions: Read the following e-mail and complete the tasks below. Remember appropriate workplace etiquette when communicating with your peers.

E-mail:

Heather,

Did you see what Christina was wearing today? It was so ugly.

Why do you think she wore that?

Also- I am so excited to go out this weekend. What are you going to wear?

Email me back!

Jennifer

Respond to the following:
Task 1: Determine why you think the e-mail is appropriate or inappropriate.
Task 2: Write a response to this e-mail.

_____

_____

_____

_____

_____

_____

_____

_____

_____

_____

Leadership and those You Supervise

You may or may not be in a position of leadership right now. If you aren't, there's bound to be a time when you are in a leadership role.

As a supervisor, your role extends beyond that of taskmaster. You are a role model, an empathetic listener, a support and an **objective** problem solver. You have the capacity to inspire and motivate your team to their highest good.

Ten tips for effective leadership:

1. Notice, compliment, and **praise** contributions
2. Help employees to find their greatness and cultivate it
3. Share responsibilities and encourage ideas
4. Validate and **empower**
5. Lead by example
6. Express appreciation
7. Maintain a positive attitude
8. Be willing to roll up your sleeves and work alongside your team
9. Be thoughtful and show you care by remembering personal details and important events
10. Listen with intention and **empathy**

> Objective: Not influenced by personal feelings or opinions in considering facts

> Praise: Express approval of

> Empower: Give someone power to do something

> Empathy: The ability to understand and share feelings of another

Cohesion: The action of performing as a united whole

Integrity: Having a moral and ethical character

Group Development: Understanding Your Team

Understanding the stages of group development can help you be a strong asset to your team. Stages naturally occur while developing **cohesion** in a group. In working with teams the middle stages can sometimes become difficult. By understand the group process you can maintain a position of **integrity** and leadership while also maintaining focus on the tasks at hand.

Forming	Groups come together
Storming	Conflict begins to arise
Norming	Agreement is reached
Performing	Group efficiently working together

Group Development: Choose Your Path

In each stage of development there are opportunities and there are pitfalls. Don't become a victim of a pitfall- instead use obstacles as an opportunity to shine! Read each of the following stages below.

1. The Forming Stage

Forming occurs in newly formed groups. Members are getting to know each other and gaining an understanding of the purpose of the meeting. Group members are mostly tentative and polite, in fear of expressing strong opinions that differ from members. Trust starts off low in the Forming Stage.

Opportunities	Pitfalls
Build relationships and trust	Members are quiet
Try to understand purpose and mission	Light interaction between members
Agree on goals	Desire to be accepted
Model accepting behavior	Not much gets accomplished

2. The Storming Stage

Much like the name reveals, conflict may occur in the Storming Stage. Group members are more comfortable, so they state their own viewpoints about issues and goals. Alliances may form, possibly to undermine the leader's role. If handled incorrectly, this stage can ruin a team from attaining the goal. Although this stage is rocky, it is an important part of group development.

Opportunities	Pitfalls
Be open to different perspectives	Ideas are criticized
Value other opinions and views	Members are judged on their viewpoints
Focus on big picture and cohesiveness	Some members focus on small problems
Embrace group culture	Personal attacks

3. The Norming Stage

Trust begins to form in the Norming Stage. The group has moved from their individual differences to cooperation for the purpose of achieving the objectives and mission. Conflict is resolved more effectively and there is also a stronger agreement on the group's common goal.

Opportunities	Pitfalls
Encourage "WE" feeling	Unwillingness to give up own ideas
Come to an agreement on rules	Unable to agree on goals
Try to support other members	Does not take responsibility
Trust team members	Does not trust team members

4. The Performing Stage

A highly effective group will reach the Performing Stage. In this stage, groups focus on useful and productive behavior, and believe the group will succeed. Sometimes smaller groups are formed within the group to make sure every team member feels involved and supported.

Opportunities	Pitfalls
Advocate problem-solving	Unwillingness to give up own ideas
Ensure everyone is involved	Unable to agree on goals
Be open to constructive criticism	Does not take responsibility
Focus on achievement	Does not trust team members

Proactively: Developing solutions in advance to deal with an expected difficulty

Reactively: Developing solutions after a problem occurs

Opposition: Resistance expressed in action or argument

Choosing the Right Language

Effective communication is important when working in a group. There is an art to how we communicate. Paying attention to the type of language we use will increase the effectiveness of communication. The language that we naturally use reflects if we are acting **proactively** or **reactively**. Proactive language sends the message of leadership and full personal responsibility. Reactive language conveys blame and lack of responsibility for one's thoughts and actions.

Reactive Language	Proactive Language
There's nothing I can do	Let's look at alternatives
That's just the way I am	I can choose a different approach
I have to do that	I will choose an appropriate response
I can't	I choose
I must	I prefer
If only	I will

By using proactive language in teamwork and meetings we can state opinions and convey **opposition** while contributing to the effectiveness of the group.

Summary

Working as a team is a shared vision. Change your "I" statements to "we" statements. Instead of thinking, "I want it to be this way," try to think, "What is the best idea for the team?" Each person in the team will have to give up a little bit of their self interest to think as a group.

As you are working with others at home, in school, at work, or with friends, keep in mind what you've learned in this module. Recognizing what you need to do to be a team player is your first step towards group success. Now it's time to implement what you know!

"A single arrow is easily broke, but not ten in a bundle." — *Japanese Proverb*

Discussion Questions

> What feeling did you get reading the reactive statements versus the proactive statements?
>
> Which reactive statements do you find yourself saying most often?

Independent Practice 1

Directions: Read the two scenarios and determine the stage of group development.

Scenario 1
A group is getting together to meet about an upcoming workshop they are creating. They need to make some important decisions to make sure the workshop runs smoothly. After the third day of meeting, the team arrives at an agreement about the vision of the workshop and the objectives to be accomplished.

Group Stage: _____

Scenario 2
This is the second day the group has met together. Everyone was pretty shy yesterday, but it is much different today. People seem to be arguing and defending their own ideas.

Group Stage: _____

Independent Practice 2

Directions: Read the following scenarios and identify the reactive statement in each. Next, change the reactive statements into proactive statements.

Scenario 1
Becky learns that her boss gave her colleague a promotion. Becky approaches her boss and says, "I can't believe you gave it to Sam."

Reactive Statement	Proactive Statement

Scenario 2
Karl's colleague asked him to help him with his presentation or an upcoming meeting. Karl answered, "There's nothing I can do to help you. I'm really busy too."

Reactive Statement	Proactive Statement

Reflect:
Explain what you did to change the reactive statements into proactive statements.

_____

_____

_____

_____

Group Activity

Directions: Complete the following tasks.

1. Form a group of 3-4 people.
2. Read the scenario.
3. Pick one of the four stages and brainstorm how you plan to act this out in the space provided.
4. Present your skit to the class and have them identify the stage.

Scenario
You are asked to create a public service announcement about the dangers of talking on your cell phone while driving.

Stage	Brainstorm

Knowledge Check

Directions: Circle the correct answer.

1. Your company has a monthly staff meeting to discuss important company issues. What is the best way to prepare for the meeting?

a) Email your supervisor anything you will be discussing prior to the meeting

b) Bring a pen and notepad

c) Obtain knowledge of key topics prior to the meeting

d) All of the above

2. Valuing _____ will help you to be open-minded when working in a group.

a) Perspective

b) Time-constraints

c) Leadership

d) Language

3. Your supervisor consistently sends you emails when she needs to communicate. What is the most appropriate mode of response?

a) To stop by her office

b) Call her cell phone

c) However is most convenient for you

d) By email

4. An example of a conversation that you might have with your supervisor would be:

a) Creating a committee to implement companywide recycling and waste reduction

b) How to operate the fax machine

c) The new relationship between two of your co-workers

d) Your divorce

5. What is proactive language?

a) Saying yes when asked to do anything

b) Volunteering for projects

c) Language that demonstrates full responsibility and leadership

d) Language that is negative, blaming or accusatory

6. In which stage of group development is it normal for conflict to erupt?

a) Perfoming

b) Forming

c) Storming

d) Norming

7. Sally states in a meeting that she "feels like she is the only one who helps out, but can't do everything." This is an example of:

a) Letting your team know how hard you work

b) Reactive communication

c) Asking for help

d) How overworked people are these days

8. Learning to work well in a team environment is important because:

a) In any field you will be working with others

b) More can be accomplished as a team

c) The outcome will be better

d) All of the above

9. To ensure group success during the Norming Stage, each individual should

a) Encourage the "we" feeling

b) Support other team members

c) Come to an agreement on common goals

d) All of the above

10. Understanding the stages of group development will help a team member better manage conflict when it arises.

a) True

b) False

Module 3

Conflict Resolution

Objectives:

- Identify and use conflict constructively

- Explain the attitudes, behaviors and strategies that help people manage conflict effectively

- Describe the appropriate steps and approaches to take when conflict occurs

Conflict Resolution

Learn to identify conflict and manage it constructively.

It is crucial to understand how to face conflict. } Interacting with others is a part of daily life and there are bound to be times when conflict will arise. Learning to identify conflict and manage it constructively will help you cultivate an efficient work environment. In this module, we will introduce you to the skills needed and teach you approaches that can be used when facing conflict.

What Do You Already Know?

Directions: Choose if each statement is true or false.

Statement	True	False
Conflict only occurs when someone is behaving badly		
It is possible to completely avoid all conflicts		
Everyone deals with conflict in the same way		

What is Conflict?

Conflict involves a struggle between people who have different ideas, values or opinions. They may also have different **expectations** or needs.

Conflict usually occurs because people have different **perceptions** of events. When people have different perceptions about the same situation, they may not be able to see eye to eye. This can lead to misunderstandings, which usually leads to conflict.

Conflict is everywhere. It can be found any time when people have different ideas, goals, and beliefs and must work together to complete a task. This can happen on the job, in the classroom or even at home. Conflict is **inevitable** and is a natural part of life. Learning to resolve conflict will help you become successful in your career.

> **Expectations:** Thoughts of what one wants to happen

> **Perceptions:** The way you view different situations

> **Inevitable:** Can't be avoided

Conflict Styles

Conflict makes most of us uncomfortable, but it is sometimes needed in order to reach a common goal. Ideally, each side has some of their needs met and is satisfied with the result.

When conflict is managed well, it offers opportunities for growth. In many cases, effective conflict resolution can make the difference between success and failure.

Conflict, when managed well, can offer growth.

It is important to note there are several different ways to respond to conflict. When you are able to recognize your own conflict style, as well as the styles of those around you, you may find a way to use it towards positive outcomes.

Common conflict styles include:

> Avoidance
> Compromise
> Collaboration
> Competition
> Accommodation

"A conflict begins and ends in the hearts and minds of people, not in the hilltops." — *Amos Oz*

Practice

Directions: Try to recognize your conflict style. Read the scenario and choose the conflict style you think you would typically use in a situation like this.

Scenario
You are a medical assistant in a hospital. As you walk into the staff room, you notice two nurses yelling at one another. Apparently they disagreed on the way the charts were filed. One of the nurses turns to you and asks, "What do you think?"

Circle the conflict style you would use in this situation.

1. Avoidance
2. Compromise
3. Collaboration
4. Competition
5. Accommodation

Assignment

Directions: Recognizing your conflict style is the first step to becoming successful in conflict resolution. Think about a conflict you've had in your life, then complete the activity below.

1. Describe the conflict.
2. How did you handle the conflict? What was the result?
3. What could you have done to better to handle the conflict?

_____

_____

_____

_____

_____

_____

Conflict Style: Avoidance

Avoidance involves ignoring a situation and waiting for it to pass. Many people believe that if they ignore a conflict, it will simply disappear. This is a "wait and see attitude." More often then not, it doesn't go away. Instead, the conflict brews until it boils over.

Quite often this is the situation when we see a great explosion over something that does not deserve that reaction. It is because the build up from trying to avoid the confrontation has now become too big to ignore.

This conflict style is the least effective. It is always best to try and communicate your perspective in an appropriate manner, rather than avoiding reality.

"Some issues are only huge if ignored."

– Amy Guth

 Discussion Questions

---

Have you ever dealt with a conflict through avoidance?

What was the outcome?

How could you have dealt with it differently?

Conflict Style: Compromise

When there is compromise, people work toward a solution that is partly acceptable to all sides. Each party gives some points to another while getting some of their own needs and wants met, known as "win-win."

When using a compromising style:

> Fairness is highly valued

> Everyone participates in give and take interactions

> Everyone is expected to give up something

The goal of compromise is for everyone to meet halfway. Unfortunately this can sometimes leave each party feeling slightly unsatisfied. However, there are times when it is necessary to compromise and be a team player. Think about the overall outcome of a compromise. It is better for everyone to have some needs met, rather than none at all.

Conflict Style: Collaboration

Collaboration is pooling of individual needs and goals towards a common goal. It is often referred to as problem-solving. Collaboration is the process of gathering an idea on top of an idea in order to come up with a creative solution to a conflict.

Collaboration involves:

> Listening to the other side

> Discussing areas of agreement and goals

> Making certain that all parties understand one another

Collaboration can sometimes be difficult to achieve because it requires each person to want to work together.

TIP: *You can encourage collaboration. Include others and let them know that their opinion matters, then come to a conclusion.*

Conflict Style: Accomodation and Competition

Two additional conflict styles are Accommodation and Competition.

Accommodation	Competition
The style of accommodation is surrendering one's own wants and needs to please someone else. This style works well in terms of customer service. However, if overused in the workplace, an individual can easily be taken advantage of and will feel unsatisfied or resentful.	In this style, individuals look at each other as competition. People practicing this style take a firm stand and know what they want, operating from a position of power. This style can be useful when there is an emergency and a decision needs to be made. However, it can be hurtful since the individual wants to succeed at another's expense.

 Assignment

---

Directions: Answer the questions that follow this scenario.

Scenario

Bill, Jane and Betsy have just been assigned a group project. It will be a challenging project, but they are certain they can complete it correctly and on time. Everyone is excited to get started. They begin by brainstorming how to divide up the task. Betsy suggests that everyone select the sections that they would like to complete, while Jane suggests that they assign sections randomly. Betsy explains that allowing everyone to do the portion they are comfortable with will produce a higher quality project. Jane does not budge, and demands that the assignment be divided at random.

At first, Bill listens to Betsy and Jane discuss the tasks. He becomes concerned that a conflict will arise, one that will make the project difficult to complete in a timely and correct fashion. He suggests that the project is split up both ways:

each member can choose one topic of their preference, while the rest are assigned randomly. In this way, they each are able to operate within their comfort level while learning about a part of the project that is outside their field of knowledge.

Betsy and Jane agree, relieved to have the conflict resolved.

Answer Bank
Collaboration
Accommodation
Avoidance
Compromise
Competition

1. Which conflict style did Bill use?_____

2. Since Betsy and Jane agreed to use Bill's suggestion, which conflict style did they both end up using?_____

3. What style do you think you would have used?_____

Solutions to Conflict
What are some things you can do to successfully resolve conflict?

> Stay flexible
> Provide an opportunity for each person to speak without criticism
> Listen to others' perspectives with respect
> Try not to get caught up in your own wants and needs
> Keep the interest of the group as your main focus
> Negotiate when working through conflict
> Accept the outcome

When keeping these strategies in mind you will be fostering a safe environment. People will feel comfortable to express their ideas and potential solutions. It will also greatly improve the likelihood that the problem can be understood. Solutions may be explored that might not otherwise have come to light.

{ **Foster a safe environment for people to feel comfortable to express their ideas.** }

Assignment

Directions: Below is an unfinished script. Read the script and choose the ending by writing the last four lines below. Your ending should reflect your understanding of conflict resolution.

Employee 1: *Hey did you take the stapler off of my desk?*

Employee 2: *Nope. I don't have your stapler.*

Employee 1: *Are you sure? You are always taking stuff off of my desk.*

Employee 2: *Yeah, take a look at my desk. It's not there.*

Employee 1:

Employee 2:

Employee 1:

Employee 2:

Discussion Question

What do you need to remember the next time conflict arises?

Limiting Conflict in the Workplace

A great way to resolve conflict is to try to foster an environment where conflict is less likely to arise.

> Develop strategies to deal with people who gossip, manipulate, show off, goof off or complain

– These pre-planned strategies will help you to work around those people and lessen the chance of a conflict

> Be yourself – Recognize your own beliefs and don't get caught up in other people's drama

> Try not to take things personally

> Ask questions when you need clarification

> Avoid physical and verbal confrontation

In conclusion, the best thing you can do is always communicate and encourage the same from others.

"The successful person has unusual skill at dealing with conflict and ensuring the best outcome for all." – *Sun Tzu*

Practice

Directions: Read each sentence and fill in the blank with the appropriate term.

is   **is not**

1. Yelling at a teammate _____ a step towards conflict resolution.

2. Having a plan to handle people who gossip or manipulate _____ a step towards conflict resolution.

3. Being polite and minding your manners _____ a step towards conflict resolution.

4. Being loud, obnoxious, and bossy _____ a step towards conflict resolution.

Summary

In this lesson, we have learned that conflict cannot always be avoided because everyone has a different point of view. However, there are ways to resolve conflict. To prepare yourself for conflict, try to pay attention to other people's conflict styles.

Remember to recognize your own typical conflict style and reflect on how you can make yourself more successful. Try to minimize the opportunity for conflict to occur in a workplace before it even happens. Learning to manage conflict will help you in both your personal and professional life.

Independent Practice 1

Directions: Read the scenario below. Sort the responses into appropriate and inappropriate responses. Then, write two additional appropriate responses you could use if placed in this situation.

Scenario
Jay and Sue work together. Jay works hard and does his job well. Sue does her job, but relies on Jay for too many things. Jay is getting fed up with pulling the weight.

Sue: *Hey Jay, how are you doing today?*

Jay: *Hey, I'm okay. Been super busy today. I feel like I can barely take a breath. How are you?*

Sue: *Oh yeah? Eh..I'm pretty slow today…just taking it easy.*

Jay: *Must be nice.*

Sue: *Yeah. Hey can you send a few reports for me? Oh, and email the guy that had some questions for us? I think I'm going to take a break.*

Jay:

| Yeah right! You're lazy. | I would, but I'm pretty busy right now. | Absolutely not! | I think we should talk about our workloads. |
| Yeah anything you need! | Let's try to balance out this work a little more. | Yes, of course. I'm not busy. | Sue, I don't mind helping, but let's try to be fair. |

Appropriate Response	Inappropriate Response

Independent Practice 2

Answer Bank
Conflict
Collaboration
Avoidance
Perception
Resolution

Directions: Read each clue and decide which term is being described. Write that term in the appropriate place in the crossword puzzle.

Across

4. Discussing ideas to make creative solution together

Down

1. The way someone views a situation

2. Determining a solution to a problem

3. A struggle between two people with different ideas

5. Ignoring a situation and waiting for it to pass

Module 3

Group Activity

Directions: Complete the following tasks.

1. Form a group of 3-4 people

2. As a group, choose one of the five conflict styles

> Avoidance
> Compromise
> Collaboration
> Competition
> Accommodation

3. Two employees want to take off the same week for vacation. Role-play what this scenario would look like using the chosen conflict style and write the pros and cons of the selected conflict style.

Conflict Style _____

Pro	Con

Knowledge Check

Directions: Circle the correct answer.

1. It is not unusual to feel a little dissatisfied when you compromise in a situation.
a) True
b) False

2. Improving your conflict resolution skills provides an opportunity for:
a) Friendships
b) Personal and professional growth
c) An uncomfortable work environment
d) None of the above

3. A good solution to conflict is to:
a) Stay flexible
a) Provide an opportunity for each person to speak without criticism
b) Negotiate when working through conflict
c) All of the above

4. Understanding how we handle conflict can help us more effectively manage conflict.
a) True
b) False

5. Conflict is inevitable.
a.) True
b.) False

6. Through knowledge about conflict styles and resolution skills, we can:
a.) Find ways to completely avoid conflict
b.) Control the outcomes of all conflict
c.) Create more conflict
d.) More effectively deal with conflict

7. When working to resolve conflict, make sure that the focus is on:
a.) Criticizing the people on the opposing side
b.) The common goal
c.) An individual and their personal life
d.) The management

8. When dealing with conflict it is okay to not be mindful of your manners.

a.) True

b.) False

9. We have learned that a win-win situation occurs when both parties in the conflict are accommodated. In order for this to happen there usually needs to be:

a.) Anger or argument

b.) One party willing to give up

c.) Compromise on both sides

d.) None of the above

10. Conflict happens when:

a.) Two people can get along with one another

b.) A manager has realistic expectations

c.) People who have different ideas, goals, and beliefs come together to accomplish a task collectively

d.) Everyone works independently

Workplace Behaviors

Module 4

Objectives:

– **Establish the foundation for a strong work ethic**

– **Create and maintain an attitude of professional excellence**

– **Conduct appropriate communication with coworkers**

Workplace Behaviors

Success means learning about professional dress, attitude, and behavior.

The path to career success takes great thought and careful planning.

Each of us hopes to find an exciting and challenging job, but getting a job is just the first step to a fulfilling career. The path to career success takes great thought and careful planning. Creating success means learning about professional dress, attitude, and behavior. This module will address how to develop and maintain workplace professionalism.

What Do You Already Know?

Directions: For each scenario, shade the best solution.

Example You are not sure how long your lunch break is at your new job.	Ask your supervisor or human resources manager to clarify.
	Take the lunch break you think you deserve.
Scenario 1 Your coworker is anxious about a challenging project that is due before the end of the day.	Offer to help with the project.
	Focus on your own work so you can go home early.
Scenario 2 Your coworker introduces a new employee from a different department.	Introduce yourself and be welcoming; offer to answer any questions that may arise.
	Introduce yourself and get back to work.
Scenario 3 Your employer assigns you a task that you find boring.	Smile and say you will get to work immediately; finish the job efficiently and thoroughly.
	Nod unenthusiastically and head back to your desk.

Establishing a Work Ethic

Ethics are values that can guide you to success. A strong work ethic will lead to excellence in the workplace. The basic foundation for a strong work ethic combines **professional etiquette**, a **pursuit of excellence**, and a **professional attitude**.

How do you present yourself? What kind of clothing do you wear to work? Do you have the right attitude? Are you communicating appropriately?

> Professional etiquette: Actions and efforts made to set you apart from the crowd

> Pursuit of excellence: Behavior that delivers a "can-do" message to employers and coworkers

> Professional attitude: Knowing what to do and when to do it in business situations

Professional Dress

A clean appearance is the first step to success in the workplace. When getting ready for work, it is a good rule to dress conservatively. It is also extremely important to maintain good hygiene and have a neat appearance. In general, clothing should look crisp and shoes should be clean and appropriate for the work environment.

A few tips:

> - Tattoos should always be covered
> - Women should use makeup sparingly, in neutral tones
> - Jewelry should be conservative and minimal
> - Any facial piercings should be removed
> - Avoid wearing perfume and cologne, especially if you work in a hospital setting

"If you want the job, you have to look the part. If you want the promotion, you have to look promotable. If you want respect, you have to dress as well or better than the industry standard." — *Susan Bixler*

Professional Interactions

Presentation extends to how you behave in your personal interactions:

> Remember to smile throughout the day
> A warm and friendly presence will create a positive first impression
> When greeting others, say hello, smile, look them in the eye, and use appropriate titles
> Introduce people by first and last names or using titles, such as Dr.
> When introduced to others, make sure that you always stand, use direct eye contact, and offer a firm handshake

Discussion Questions

Should you greet the president of your company the same way you would greet a new employee?

Why or why not?

Practice

Directions: Put a check mark next to the characteristics that best describe an employee with a strong work ethic.

Volunteers for less appealing projects	
Finishes work very quickly in order to sneak out of the office early	
Tries to know everyone's names and titles at the workplace	
Arrives early to work and eagerly begins the day	
Spends time working on a second job while at work	
Covers up tattoos while at work	
Chooses to dress appropriately at work	

Assignment

Directions: List five things you can do to develop a strong work ethic below.

1.

2.

3.

4.

5.

Professional Reputation

Pursuing excellence is another way to earn the respect of your coworkers and upper management. A reputation for excellence will establish you as both a leader and a team player.

> Show up on time, if not early
> Learn everyone's name
> Help new employees learn the ropes
> Let others know that you are willing to help in projects
> Keep your work environment clean and use office supplies appropriately
> Do you best work, even when no one is looking
> Be consistent and detail-oriented
> Treat your coworkers with respect and kindness

By establishing an excellent reputation you will be considered responsible and dependable. In a recent survey, 75% of employers cited responsibility and dependability as the most important qualities for hiring and promotion. If you want to be someone who can be counted on, show up every day on time, finish your work before leaving for the day, and do the little things that no one else wants to do.

Discussion Questions

When you are punctual, responsible, kind, and dependable, what kind of example do you set for new employees?

What kind of reputation do you plan to reinforce for the company?

Practice

Directions: Choose if each action represents a professional or unprofessional attitude. Write the actions in the correct spaces below.

Arrive on time for work	Dress neatly, in clean clothing	Treat coworkers with respect	Meet future deadlines consistently
Leave the office early to avoid being asked about a late project	Trade projects with coworkers in order to work on tasks that are more fun and interesting	Push paperwork into a drawer to give the impression of neatness	Buy the boss lunch to apologize for unprofessional behavior

Unprofessional Attitude	Professional Attitude

Professional Attitude

Maintaining a professional, positive attitude is critical to workplace success. So many people find it hard to keep a positive outlook about work. Small adjustments in attitude can have a huge effect on your output. Just smiling at a colleague and offering encouragement may alter the course of the project toward a successful completion. Also, stay open-minded about your tasks when communicating with colleagues. Attitude is a reflection of how a person sees himself. Positive thinking will spread to others and create energy. That energy will carry through the workplace and stimulate production. This will greatly enhance your workplace experience.

"Nothing can stop the man with the right mental attitude from achieving his goal; nothing on earth can help the man with the wrong mental attitude." — *Thomas Jefferson*

Professional Communication

Communication, like any skill, takes practice. The best communicators are articulate and thoughtful. Professional communication requires that you be friendly, assertive, and clear. Remember, every interaction you have is an opportunity to practice communication skills.

> Smile and use eye contact — we are drawn to friendly people
> Listen and be careful not to talk too much
> Ask questions — remember, people like to talk about themselves
> Be interested and show that you care
> Use your body language and tone of voice to express interest and enthusiasm
> Focus on the body language of your audience — a large percentage of communication is nonverbal
> Be assertive and show confidence
> Be clear and concise — others will see you as respectful of their time

Discussion Questions

> What does a lack of eye contact communicate to your audience?
>
> How might someone interpret crossed arms or foot tapping?
>
> How do you feel when someone takes a long time to get to the point of a conversation?

Core Professional Values

Each of us has **values** that shape our behavior. We bring these values to everything we do, including our actions in the workplace. Each of these values can enhance our performance and help build our careers.

Core values that can be used in the business world include:

- Accountability
- Collaboration
- Consistency
- Efficiency
- **Innovation**
- **Integrity**
- Leadership
- Passion
- Quality
- Respect

Values: Ideas or beliefs that shape our ideas of right and wrong

Innovation: The creation of better ideas, products, or processes

Integrity: Using honesty and truthfulness in your decisions and actions

Discussion Questions

> Reflect on situations in your life when you've used these core values.
>
> How did you apply these concepts?
>
> How can that experience help you in the workplace?

Personal Integrity

Consistent integrity is vital to career success. Your actions, methods, principles, expectations, and outcomes should be constant. You must listen to that little voice in your head that says whether your actions are right or wrong.

Honesty is a major part of integrity. Being truthful with colleagues and supervisors is necessary for a productive and successful workplace. The business suffers when people begin to deceive one another.

 **Assignment**

Directions: Complete the following tasks.

Task 1: Write your own definition for "integrity."

Task 2: Describe three ways you can show integrity in a workplace environment.

 **Practice**

Directions: Below are some common workplace situations. Place a check mark next to the situation where the employee <u>lacks</u> professional integrity.

Taking credit for someone else's work	
Answering phone calls, e-mails, or other forms of communication within 24 hours	
Asking a colleague to punch your timecard at closing time so you can leave one hour early	
Staying late to finish a project by the deadline	
Calling in sick when you want to go to the beach	
Providing feedback, both positive and negative, about a coworker's participation on a project	

Independent Practice 1

Directions: Pick three core values from the list below and write a sentence or two on how you would demonstrate that value in the workplace.

| Integrity | Respect | Leadership | Accountability | Collaboration |

Efficiency	*Completing a project in a timely fashion*

Independent Practice 2

Directions: Reflect on what you have learned in this module. Write down two things you feel you do well and two areas where you think you need to improve. Reflect on your professional communication, professional reputation, core professional values, etc. Honesty is a major part of integrity, so be honest with yourself.

_____
_____
_____
_____
_____
_____
_____
_____
_____
_____
_____
_____
_____
_____
_____
_____
_____
_____
_____

Group Activity

Directions: Working with your group, come up with two appropriate ways to handle each given situation. Choose one situation to perform for the class.

Situation 1: *You are introduced to a new coworker. You:*

Situation 2: *You are running late to work and need to dress quickly for a casual day at the office. You should grab:*

Situation 3: *You are assigned a boring yet important task. You:*

Situation 4: *Karen, your coworker, needs help editing a report she wrote. She asks you for help. You say:*

Knowledge Check

Directions: Circle the correct answer.

1. What are ethics?

a.) Disrespectful behavior

b.) Values and standards

c.) Forms of discipline

d.) Financial timelines

2. It is a good idea to dress conservatively when choosing attire for work.

a.) True

b.) False

3. In a recent survey, _____% of employers cited responsibility and dependability as the most important qualities that they look for when hiring and promoting their employees.

a.) 50

b.) 80

c.) 35

d.) 75

4. Your positive attitude toward coworkers and projects can _____ others.

a.) Distract

b.) Discourage

c.) Encourage

d.) Irritate

5. Integrity requires

a.) Assertiveness

b.) Greed

c.) Cleanliness

d.) Honesty

6. When you are working on a group project, it is acceptable to put in less effort than your coworkers; they will pick up the slack.

a.) True

b.) False

7. A smile can change the course of your coworker's day.

a.) True

b.) False

8. Good communicators

a.) Talk more than they listen

b.) Use reflective listening

c.) Interrupt in order to correct false or inaccurate information

d.) Cross their arms to demonstrate authority

9. What should you do if a coworker is running 15 minutes late and asks you to clock him in?

a.) Clock him in

b.) Inform your boss immediately

c.) Explain to your coworker that it wouldn't be right to clock him in but ask if there is any other way you can help

d.) Pull the fire alarm

10. In order to dress professionally at work, an individual should:

a.) Cover tattoos

b.) Avoid wearing perfume or cologne

c.) Only wear conservative jewelry, if any

d.) All of the above

Module 5

Job Search Skills

Objectives:

- **Identify the qualities valued by a future employer**

- **Demonstrate how to capitalize on your strengths**

- **Formulate how to effectively prepare for your interview**

Job Search Skills

Strengthen your job search skills.

Research resources, network and practice strategies.

Searching for a job goes beyond filling out applications and résumés. There is a lot you can do while still in school to reach the career you desire. In this module, you will strengthen your job search skills and learn how to research important resources, network efficiently, and practice strategies for contacting organizations.

What Do You Already Know?

Directions: Put a check mark next to the tasks that should be completed when you are conducting a job search.

___ Research opportunities ___ Contact professional organizations

___ Attend job fairs ___ Conduct informational interviews

___ Consider volunteer work or an externship ___ Network to make connections

Define What You're Looking for

Take a moment to define the career you are working toward...

> What's the specific job you are working toward?
> In which cities would you like to work?
> What type of schedule would you be willing to work?

There's a lot you can do to help your job hunt even before you send out applications and résumés. Take an active role in your career and take advantage of the resources you have to help reach your career goals.

"Trust yourself. You know more than you think you do." — *Benjamin Spock*

Facilitate: To help bring about

Mentor: A trusted counselor or guide

Get Involved — Use Your Resources

Although you may not realize it, you have resources at your fingertips. There are multiple organizations created solely for individuals in search of jobs. Search to see what resources are available to you and take advantage of them.

Two major resources offering career support for individuals are:

Career Services Office

Your school's career services department provides services to students to assist with job placement upon graduation. The resources available through this office can help you develop your own job search plan, **facilitate** important relationships, and assist with writing and reviewing your résumé.

Professional interest Groups and Organizations

There are professional groups for almost all career fields. These groups are simply for individuals who are interested in and/or work in the same field. Joining a professional group is a great way to get started in your career. You will have the opportunity to make professional connections and find **mentors**. Utilize the benefits of these organizations, participate in meetings and events, meet new people, and get involved!

TIP: *Use the Internet to search for professional interest groups or organizations.*

Networking

Many people find jobs because "they know someone" in the field. This is commonly known as networking. If you have ever followed up on a job tip you received from a family member or a friend, you have networked. Think of networking as getting to know people. Every person you meet is someone you are networking with.

How to Network:

> Take an interest in new people you meet
> Find out who knows whom
> Invite people out for social events
> Be generous and help others network
> Follow up with your contacts
> Tap into your network

As you continue through school and meet new people, view situations through the lens of networking. Networking could be the key to help you land the job you desire.

 ## Assignment

Directions: Complete the following tasks.

1. Take 5 minutes to list people you know, including relatives, friends, instructors, and others in your field.

2. Write down as many phone numbers and e-mail addresses that you know.

3. Contact five of these individuals and tell them about your career aspirations.

4. Try to contact at least two people a day. You may be pleasantly surprised with the outcome of this exercise!

Name	Phone Number	E-mail

Research Other Opportunities

Become familiar with the field and the opportunities available to help you reach your goal. Research the Internet, newspapers, and postings at your school to locate more opportunities to network.

In addition to utilizing your school's career services office and joining professional organizations, there are other ways to extend your network and help your job search. Seek out and participate in these types of opportunities.

TIP: *Make it a goal to attend a career fair, join a social media group, and volunteer.*

Read about these opportunities:

Career Fairs	Social Media Networking	Volunteering
What: Fairs for employers, recruiters, and schools to meet with prospective job seekers **Why:** Provides opportunitites to make connections with recuriters and organizations in your field	**What:** Websites allowing individuals to research and connect with professionals in their field **Why:** Offers an oppportunity for you to meet people you may not have met face-to-face **Example:** LinkedIn	**What:** Contributing your time and effort to an organization or company **Why:** A great way to practice skills, meet potential employers, and help build your network

# Assignment

Directions: Create a personal commercial that sells your skills and ties into your field. Use the steps below to write a brief statement about yourself as if it were a commercial. This commercial can be used when meeting new people.

Step 1: Introduce yourself. Highlight your skills and strengths. Include your career aspiration, education, and qualifications.

Step 2: Define what type of job you are looking for. Sell yourself!

Step 3: Practice your commercial by reading it aloud to yourself or to a friend!

_____

_____

_____

_____

_____

_____

_____

_____

_____

_____

_____

_____

_____

_____

 **Practice**

Directions: Think about whether each method below is an effective or an ineffective form of networking. Write each in the appropriate column.

| Visit as many groups as possible | Leave it up to chance | E-mail your contacts every day | Hold volunteer positions |
| Only focus on important people in the field | Attend career fairs | Pay it foward — help others network | Make constant requests |

Effective	Ineffective

Appropriate Electronic Representation

As you are networking and reaching out to opportunities, think about how you represent yourself on the Internet. Employers and people in your professional network will pay attention to how you portray yourself on social media sites, such as Facebook and Twitter. Think to yourself, "Is my profile appropriate for everyone to see, including people in my professional network?"

Make sure your profile is free of the following:

> Pictures at parties
> Profanity
> Inappropriate conversations

Your e-mail address is also an important piece to represent yourself professionally. Your e-mail should be comprised of your name, initials, birthday, or a combination of these items.

Remember, your e-mail address is a first impression.

Appropriate	Inappropriate
JSmith@yahoo.com	xxxpartygirl@gmail.com
JSmith84@gmail.com	cuti345987@yahoo.com
JonSmith@hotmail.com	funkychicken@hotmail.com

Identify Leads and Opportunities

Your research will lead you to dozens of opportunities. Narrow your search to make sure you spend your time wisely. The best opportunities are those that will support you in your job search.

For every **potential** opportunity, locate the following information:

> Potential: Having the capacity to develop into something in the future

> Name of the organization or office
> Contact information
> Mission statement and/or purpose
> Workshops or meetings you can attend
> Available services
> Benefits for members, if there's a membership

Make it a goal to locate this information for a few opportunities a week. You can never be too connected!

Discussion Question

How can I take advantage of the opportunities around me?

Practice

Directions: Review the flyer of a fictional professional organization on the right, then fill out the chart below.

Name	
Mission	
Services	

Module 5

Contact and Follow-Up

You can research and network all you'd like, but it won't do any good if you don't take action. After researching and identifying leads, contact the organization or individual. The best method of contact is to make a phone call. As a second option, you can send an e-mail.

Follow these steps when making initial contact:

1. Introduce yourself and your interest in the field
2. Explain how you located the opportunity
3. Ask how you can become involved
4. Listen **attentively**
5. Thank them for their time

You may not be able to speak with someone right away. If this is the case, leave a message and follow up if you don't hear back within a few days. To follow up, call or e-mail a few days later mentioning you are "following up" on your request. Remember to always be polite!

TIP: *When making contact, be sure to speak clearly and rehearse what you say.*

> Attentive: Paying close attention to something or someone

Discussion Question

> Why do you think a follow-up call with someone you contact is recommended?

Informational Interview

Another powerful job search tool is an informational interview. This **proactive** approach to your job search will help you gain information about different jobs and organizations.

> Proactive: Initiating change, rather than reacting to events

To conduct an informational interview:

1. Make a list of people you know who may know of or work for an organization you are interested in.

2. Choose a few individuals from the list and call to request an appointment.

3. Prepare a list of questions that will not only help you learn more about the company and its available job opportunities, but may also help you meet additional **referrals**.

4. Meet and interview the employee. After the meeting, make sure to thank them! It's also a good idea to send a follow-up note, thanking them for their time and insight.

> Referrals: People who, after meeting you, pass along your contact information and recommend you to others

Use the detailed information sheet on page 92 about planning for your information interview. Tear out the sheet and save the copy.

Pave a Road to Success!

Networking Tools: Preparing for Your Informational Interview

"Where do you see yourself in five years?"
A powerful tool for paving a road to success begins with a visualization exercise. Close your eyes and imagine where you see yourself five years from now. What type of position do you hold? What job duties are you responsible for? Not only will this technique prepare you for an interview, but it can also help you head in the right direction as you begin your job search campaign.

Make a List of People You Know
Once you have decided upon your professional path of interest, make a list of all of the people you know that may be able to help you reach your goals. Choose those who can help you connect to other people within a company or an industry. Creating a list is an important part of networking.

Call and Make an Appointment
Call to set up a 15-to-30-minute informational interview regarding your contact's specialty. Most people will be more than happy to help you, but don't get discouraged if you find that some people are too busy to commit to an appointment.

Create an Agenda in Preparation for Your Meeting
This is your meeting. Don't assume the person will give you the information you need unless you ask the right questions. Select questions that will give you the most information.

Present the Professional You
Dress to impress — dress and act for the role of the position you are seeking. Learn as much as possible about the company before the interview so you can ask informed questions and demonstrate that you are prepared.

Convey Appreciation and Interest
Display your interest and show you are impressed. Say something like, "I was given your number and told you are considered to be an expert in your field. How did you get started?"

Be Prepared to Answer Questions About You
Prepare a short personal statement that you can present if you're asked about your job search. Bring a résumé, but don't offer it unless requested. Remember, this type of interview is just about getting information.

Network and Get Referred
Don't be afraid to ask for other contacts in the field. If no names are suggested, be grateful for information or suggestions obtained. Take advantage of the referrals you receive and take action.

Be Sure to Send Thank-You and Follow-Up Letters
Thank the person at the conclusion of the interview, but also send a letter or e-mail stating your gratitude for the time given.

 **Assignment**

Directions: Now that you have reviewed the steps needed to prepare for your informational interview, use the space provided to brainstorm the following two questions.

1. Who do you know that may work for a company or business you would like to learn more about?

   _____
   _____
   _____
   _____
   _____
   _____

2. What questions would you want to prepare in advance of meeting with a contact at a company you are interested in working for?

   _____
   _____
   _____
   _____
   _____
   _____

Thinking Ahead

Although a large part of your job search will likely involve networking, completing a few additional tasks will help you be prepared once you land that all-important first interview.

> Reference list: A list of people who can speak to your character and capabilities

Continue working on your résumé, compile a **reference list**, and gather important documents. Keep a collection of observations from instructors, work examples, and any certificates. Ask for letters of recommendation from instructors while you're still in school. You may want to prepare a well-organized portfolio of these items and be ready to share them during an interview.

The success of your job search is directly related to the actions you take. Utilize the resources available to you, and don't wait until graduation day to get involved. Early preparation and planning will give you the best chance to land a great job!

"The best way to predict the future is to create it." — *Abraham Lincoln*

Independent Practice 1

Directions: Match the correct term to its definition. Write the term in the space provided.

Professional Organizations	Networking	Career Service Office
Follow Up	Career Fairs	Informational Interview

Helps students develop job search strategies, facilitate important relationships, and create strategic career decisions	
Fairs for employers, recruiters, and schools to meet with prospective job seekers	
A proactive approach that will help you gain information about different jobs and organizations	
Use personal connections to learn about potential jobs	
Groups for individuals who are interested and/or work in the same field	
If you haven't heard back from an organization, contact them after a few days	

Independent Practice 2

Directions: Read the following scenario and complete the chart below. Think about the tasks Sam did correctly or incorrectly.

Scenario

While in his last quarter of school, Sam started to think about the next step — getting a job. He remembered noticing a flyer posted at his school's career service office about a career fair. Sam learned about career fairs and thought it could be a good way to meet potential employers. The next day Sam went to the fair. He made sure to dress appropriately in clean slacks and a nice shirt to look presentable. When he arrived at the fair he saw dozens of booths representing different organizations and services. He approached several booths, listened to the representatives attentively, and spoke about his own capabilities. A few people asked for his résumé, but, unfortunately, he had forgotten to bring copies. He left the fair with multiple business cards and a better idea of the organizations involved in his field. Sam hoped he would hear from some of the people he met that afternoon.

Attended a career fair	Didn't bring any résumés to hand out	Waited until last quarter to start thinking about his career
Communicated and received contacts from several groups	Made sure his appearance was presentable	Relied on organizations to contact him instead of using it

Correct	Incorrect

Module 5

 **Group Activity**

Directions: Complete the following tasks.

1. Form a group of 3 to 4 people.

2. Have each person in the group choose one topic to research at the Career Services office.

3. Visit your school's Career Services office either as a group or on your own.

4. Gather together as a group and review all the materials you retrieved. Create a poster about what your school's Career Services office can offer students on your campus.

Topics to research:

1. Résumé Assistance

2. Externship Information

3. General Information about Careers

4. Upcoming Career Fairs

5. Professional Career Organizations

Knowledge Check

Directions: Circle the correct answer.

1. Extend your network by participating in
a.) Career fairs
b.) Social media networking
c.) Volunteer work
d.) All of the above

2. It is recommended to conduct a few informational interviews while working on your job search.
a.) True
b.) False

3. Your school's Career Services Office is a great resource, providing you with
a.) Job search strategies
b.) Important contacts in your field
c.) Assistance to create strategic career decisions
d.) All of the above

4. If you have ever followed up on a job tip you received from a family member or a friend, you have successfully applied networking skills.
a.) True
b.) False

5. To network appropriately, you should do all but the following
a.) Tap into your network
b.) Take interest in new people you meet
c.) Expect someone to get you a job
d.) Be generous and help others network

6. It's also important to start gathering _____ while working on your job search.
a.) Work samples
b.) Letters of recommendation
c.) Observations from instructors
d.) All of the above

7. When you initially contact an organization, follow these steps for an effective phone call

a.) Introduce yourself and explain your interest in the field; Explain the requirements you are looking for in a career; Ask if you can meet them today

b.) Introduce yourself and explain your interest in the field; Explain how you located the opportunity; Ask how you can become involved

c.) Explain how you located the opportunity; Ask if you can interview them right now; See if they could meet you today

d. None of the above

8. An example of an appropriate way to follow up on a lead is to

a.) Call a few days later and leave a polite voice mail

b.) Show up at the organization without prior notification

c.) E-mail people in the company every day until someone responds

d.) Casually call the organization, frustrated you haven't heard back, and demand an answer

9. You don't need to start thinking about looking for a job until you've finished school.

a.) True

b.) False

10. An effective way to research for professional interest groups or organizations is to

a.) Search the Internet

b.) Ask people in your network for recommendations

c.) Visit your school's Career Services Office and ask for information

d.) All of the above

Module 6

Interview Preparation

Objectives:

- Identify the qualities valued by a future employer

- Demonstrate how to capitalize on your strengths

- Formulate how to effectively prepare for your interview

Interview Preparation

Have a plan in place for interviews.

With tips and careful prep work, going to an interview can be simple.

Many people find the interview process to be nerve racking. This doesn't have to be the case. With tips and careful prep work, going on an interview can be simple. By identifying the factors that will impress a potential employer, you can have a plan in place for interviews with any company. This module will provide insight into planning for the interview process.

What Do You Already Know?

Directions: Place a check mark next to appropriate steps you can take to prepare for an interview.

Steps — Is this appropriate?	Yes	No
Research the history of the company where you will be interviewing		
Find out the interviewer's home address and personal contact information		
E-mail everyone in the company to tell them you are looking forward to the interview		
Think of your strengths and weaknesses and be prepared to discuss both		
Rehearse questions to ask your interviewer		

What are Employers Looking for?

Employers look for more than just job-specific skills when they are filling a position. They look for certain **attributes** in addition to job skills.

These attributes include:

> A diverse set of communication skills
> Interpersonal skills
> Problem-solving skills
> **Flexibility**
> Ability to learn quickly
> **Computer literacy**
> Motivation
> **Resourcefulness**
> Creativity and **vision**
> **Accountability**
> A clean appearance

Attributes: A feature regarded as a characteristic

Flexibility: Showing capability to adapt to new, different, or changing requirements

Computer Literacy: Knowledge and ability to use computers or other related technology

Resourcefulness: Capable of devising ways to meet situations

Vision: The act or power of imagination

Accountability: A willingness to accept responsiblity and follow through

How to Communicate

It is a good idea for job applicants to practice their communication skills. Successful communication is clear, direct, correct, and polite.

Be sure that:

> Your message is clear and concise
> You know exactly what you are trying to say
> You know why you want to share the message
> You stick to the point
> You speak in the proper tone

Employers want to see that you can express yourself clearly when speaking and writing. They also want to make sure you can listen well to others.

Discussion Questions

Can you think of someone whose messages are hard to understand?

What makes their messages so difficult for you to follow?

What can you do to avoid that person's mistakes?

Interpersonal Skills

Employers also look for **interpersonal skills**. These are the behaviors and feelings that are inside of us. They affect how we work together and communicate with other people, how well we listen, and our attitudes toward others and our work.

Having good interpersonal skills is the ability to do the following:

> Interpersonal skills: Commonly referred to as people skills

- > Work well with others
- > Relate to your coworkers
- > Motivate those around you
- > Ease conflict

Employers are looking for people who can become part of a team and work together with others to get a job done. Having good interpersonal skills is a must for many employers.

Problem Solving

Problem solving is the ability to view a problem differently in order to come up with a solution. This requires you to think creatively to find solutions to problems. You need to be able to use your creativity, thinking skills, and past experiences, along with available information, to solve problems.

Communication, interpersonal skills, and problem solving are common skills employers seek. It is important to have a good understanding of these attributes along with specific skills when trying to land a position. Not only will it make you more appealing to prospective employers, but it will help you to stand out among the many competing applicants.

Discussion Questions

> In your experience, what have you done to solve a problem?
>
> What steps did you take?

Learning your Strengths

A common interview question is "What are your strengths?" Even though it is routinely asked, it is one of the most difficult questions to answer.

When the interviewer asks an applicant to talk about their strengths and weaknesses, they usually want to hear how those strengths relate to the position. It will be helpful to prepare for this question by assessing your own skills.

How do you determine your strengths?

> Review your current skills, talents, weaknesses, abilities, and interests
> Start by looking at any accomplishments or achievements that you are proud of
> Think about what strengths, skills, or personal qualities you used to accomplish the achievements
> Recall any problems you encountered and what steps you took to overcome them

Try This: Assignment

Directions: Achievements can be any obstacle you've overcome. Answer the following questions.

1. Write a list of your achievements and briefly describe each.

_____
_____
_____
_____

2. Choose one of your achievements and describe the steps it took to complete the tasks, including any obstacles and coworkers involved.

_____
_____
_____
_____

3. Which traits did you use to accomplish this task?

_____
_____
_____
_____

Continue the same process for other achievements from your list. Reflecting on your achievements and traits will help you to prepare for any interview.

Practice

Directions: Use the answer bank to fill in the blanks.

Answer Bank
strengths
weaknesses
research
attributes
prepared

1. A great way to prepare is to learn about the company through _____.

2. You are sure to ace the interview if you are well organized and _____.

3. Try to play your _____ down when you are interviewing for a job.

4. During an interview, you should highlight your _____.

5. Problem solving and communication skills are _____ that you should mention during your interview.

Common Interview Questions

Although all job interviews are different, the types of questions you will answer will be similar. Most companies want the same type of employee: someone who is motivated, resourceful, and able to work well with others. The questions they ask will help them find out how you will fit in with their company and knowing these questions will help. Below you will find some commonly asked interview questions.

> Tell me a little bit about yourself.
> What do you know about this organization?
> Who are our competitors?
> Why do you want to work here?
> What are your strengths? What are your weaknesses?
> How would your former boss/coworkers describe you?
> Where do you see yourself in 5 years?
> How do you handle pressure?
> Tell me about your greatest work-related accomplishment.
> Tell me about an obstacle you faced at work or in school, and how you handled it.
> Can you explain any gaps in your résumé?
> How will your experience translate into success in this job?

TIP: *Come back to these questions so you can practice your answers later.*

Interview the Interviewer

You should be ready to answer some challenging questions. At the end of your interview, you will have the chance to ask your own questions. Be prepared to take advantage of this opportunity! Presenting questions will show that you have prepared and put thought into the interview beforehand.

Try to ask questions that show the interviewer that you've done your homework and researched the company. Do not ask about salary or compensation; that is information for a later interview, when you are a serious candidate for the job.

As a starting point, consider the following list:

> What are the greatest challenges the company is facing right now?
> What is this organization's plan for growth?
> What do you enjoy about YOUR job?
> How should I follow up with you?

 **Assignment**

Directions: Sometimes it is good to get another perspective when preparing for an interview. In this scenario, you will be the hiring manager for the position you want. Write down your answers below.

1. Describe the kind of employee that would be best for the position.
(Think about the traits and skills you would need.)

_____

_____

2. What questions would you ask?

_____

_____

3. Take a moment to determine what qualities you possess and which ones you need to work on or develop.

_____

_____

Practice

Directions: Review the following questions and decide whether they would be appropriate to ask on an initial job interview. Write them in the correct column. Initial job interview questions:

> How long have you been with this company?
> How long of a lunch break do I get?
> Do I have to work with others if I want to take this job?
> What kind of person is ideal for this job?
> Can you describe the work environment?
> Can I leave early if I finish my work before closing time?

Appropriate Questions	Inappropriate Questions

Preparing through Research

Perhaps the biggest mistake you can make when heading to an interview is being underprepared. This can make the difference between getting an offer and getting rejected.

How can you prepare for an interview?

> Start by researching the company
> **Gather and read through as much information as possible about the company or organization**
> Visit the company's website to learn about the history, leadership, and headquarters of the company
> **Find out who will interview you**
> Learn about the corporate culture of the company

Gathering information will help you relate your past successful experience with the needs of the organization.

Knowing if you will be meeting with a human resources manager or a direct supervisor is important in order for you to be better prepared.

Conducting research will help you to avoid asking questions that can be easily answered. It will also show your interviewer that you have excellent research and preparation skills.

TIP: *The Internet is a great tool to learn about the company — research the company and its employees. Search through the company website, and research it through reviews and professional networking sites.*

Mentally and Physically Prepare

You can never underestimate the power of a good first impression. Once you have done the research and have a solid understanding of the nature of the business, its history, leadership, and corporate culture, you should focus on mentally preparing for the job interview.

> Review your strengths, weaknesses, and achievements

> Prepare intelligent answers to common questions

   What are your strengths and weaknesses?

   Why do you want to work here?

   Why should we hire you?

> Rehearse your responses

   Doing a mock interview with a friend or mentor is good practice and will help to build your self-confidence

> Compose questions to ask the interviewer

Being physically prepared will also help to make the best possible first impression.

> Make sure to wear appropriate attire to the interview
> It is better to be overdressed than underdressed
> Your clothes should be neat and clean
> You should be well groomed

TIP: *Plan your outfit at least the day before the interview. Try it on to make sure it fits correctly and doesn't have wrinkles. Make sure it will give the right impression.*

Knowing the Details

It is important to get all of the details organized before an interview to be as prepared as possible. Preparing for every detail will ease your mind in the time leadingup to the interview.

Details to consider:

> Know where you are going and what to bring
> Get the names and titles of the individuals who will conduct the interview
> Find the company's contact information in case you need to reach them
> Ask for the address of the location of where the interview will be held
> Map the directions and be certain that you know where you are going
> See how long it will take to get there by doing a trial run and considering traffic conditions

 **Discussion Question**

What are the details I need to gather before going to the interview?

When You Arrive

> Arrive fifteen minutes early
> Bring a copy of your résumé and refer to it during the interview
> Greet your interviewer by name with a firm handshake
> Speak properly and use good manners with everyone that you meet
> Be enthusiastic and show interest with the use of body language, eye contact, and a positive attitude

Summary

When you spend the extra time preparing for an interview by researching the company and making sure you are mentally and physically prepared, you will be the most successful in an interview. Remember to always follow up with a handwritten note to your interviewer to thank them for their time, leaving a positive lasting impression of a potential employee.

Independent Practice 1

Directions: Prepare your answers to the following interview questions. Write your answers in the spaces provided.

1. Tell me a little bit about yourself.

_____

_____

_____

2. What are your strengths?

_____

_____

_____

3. What are your weaknesses?

_____
_____
_____

4. What motivates you?

_____
_____
_____

5. How would your former boss and coworkers describe you?

_____
_____
_____

6. Where do you see yourself in five years?

_____
_____
_____

7. Talk about your greatest work-related accomplishment.

_____
_____
_____

8. Talk about a time when you went above and beyond for a project.

_____
_____
_____

Independent Practice 2

Directions: The following items must be located in order to be prepared for your interview. This will require some research, but the answers will help you to make a great impression. If you are not currently interviewing for a position, choose a large, well-known company and use them for research purposes. Record some notes from your research in the spaces below.

A brief history of the company	
The company's headquarters	
The number of people the company employs	
The name of the current president/CEO	
The name and position of your interviewer	
The company's reputation	
The last time the company was in the news	
Specific directions to the interview location	

Group Activity

Directions: Complete the following tasks:

1. Form a group of 3 to 4 people.

2. Imagine you are in a job interview and the interviewer asks you about your strengths.

3. Write an example of how you would answer this question in a clear, concise way and write an example of a difficult-to-understand answer.

4. Pick two examples from your group and present them to the class. Have the class decide which example was clear and which example was difficult to understand.

Difficult to Understand	Clearly Communicated

Knowledge Check

Directions: Circle the correct answer.

1. Employers are only looking for specific jobs skills when interviewing a potential candidate for a job.

a.) True

b.) False

2. An applicant's interpersonal skills are not important to future employers.

a.) True

b.) False

3. Effective communication includes all the following except

a.) Proper grammar

b.) Correct spelling

c.) Short message

d.) Fancy letterhead

4. Being a good problem solver requires all the following except

a.) Being creative

b.) Being closed-minded

c.) Use of past experiences and available information to solve problems

d.) The ability to view a problem from different angles

5. What you wear to an interview is not important.

a.) True

b.) False

6. Preparing for an interview does not include

a.) Researching the company

b.) Mapping the best route to the interview location

c.) Bringing along a friend for moral support

d.) Preparing answers to common questions

7. You should bring a copy of your résumé to an interview for your own reference.

a.) True

b.) False

8. Body language during an interview can be used to convey

a.) Your education

b.) Your interest

c.) Your prior experience

d.) How well you will perform the job duties

9. Asking prepared questions during an interview shows

a.) That you spent time getting ready for the interview

b.) That you are interested in the position

c.) That you have done research about the company

d.) All of the above

10. You only need to send a thank-you note once you are hired.

a.) True

b.) False

Module 7

Customer Service

Objectives:

- **Define quality customer service**

- **Describe methods for dealing with difficult or indifferent customers**

- **Practice an ethic of excellence in customer service**

Customer Service

Execute an ethic of excellence in customer service.

A unique style to promote success.

In this module, you'll learn characteristics of quality customer service, methods for dealing with difficult customers, and how to execute an ethic of excellence in delivering customer service. Combined, these habits will allow you to create a responsive, caring approach to customer service. As you read about how customer service works, you'll transform what you learn into your own unique style to promote your organization and your individual success as an employee.

What Do You Already Know?

Who are your customers?

Directions: Imagine yourself in the following job-related situations. Check the box next to the individual you interact with if you believe that person is your customer.

Job Setting	Individual	Is this person your customer? Yes	No
Medical Office	Drug Rep		
Retail Store	Store Manager		
Corporate Security Office	Building Visitor		
Grocery Store	Delivery Person		
Hotel	Business Traveler		

What is Customer Service?

Customer service is the lifeblood of any business or workplace. It plays a major role in an organization's ability to create income and revenue. A customer service experience can, for better or worse, change a client's view of your whole organization. Therefore, customer service is important to all types of work.

The guiding rule of good customer service is, "You will be judged by what you do, not what you say." Leave your customers raving about their experience! Excellent customer service should be a top priority in everything we say and do.

Discussion Question

> Think about a time that you had great customer service.
>
> How did it make you feel?

Four Characteristics of Quality Customer Service

Characteristic #1: Be Present

To give good customer service, it is important to be aware and present. Employees should focus on the customer, their actions, and the entire situation.

Take the time to identify customer needs by listening, **paraphrasing**, and asking questions. Pay attention to what the customer is really saying. Listen to words and tone of voice, noting body language and feelings. Be careful not to think you automatically know what the customer wants.

> **Paraphrasing:** Restating the customer's words to ensure you heard his concerns and feelings

"His tone of voice sounds worried."

"I really need to listen to what he is saying."

"I wonder how I can make him more comfortable."

Characteristic #2: Be Proactive

Customers don't just buy products and services. They also buy good feelings and solutions to problems. Most customer needs are **emotional**. The more you know your customers, the better you are able to **anticipate** their needs. Anticipating your customers' needs will allow you to go beyond their expectations.

> Emotional: Mental state or feeling associated with an evaluation of our experiences

> Anticipate: To guess or become aware of a situation and prepare to take action

- Communicate regularly with your customers
- Recognize your customers' needs instead of waiting for them to present a problem
- Make an extra effort

A spirit of kindness and generosity will produce an ethic of excellence resulting in a memorable experience for your customers, which they will communicate to others.

Read the following scenario and underline examples of where Joey demonstrates characteristics of quality customer service.

Scenario

Joey is a great employee because he practices great customer service. He lets his customers finish speaking before he responds. He repeats their concerns back to his customers in his own words, so he can be sure he understands them. He continues to smile and make eye contact with customers, no matter what the request. A human connection is very important to good customer service, and this is where Joey shines. He's proactive with the customers, and that makes him fantastic for the company.

Characteristic #3: Build Trust by Making Promises You Can Keep

Building trust and relationships is a large part of customer service. To build trust, be helpful, **courteous**, **reliable**, and knowledgeable. If you say, "I will call you back later today," make sure you follow through. Otherwise, don't say it. Think before you make any promise — nothing harms customers more than a broken promise.

> Courteous: Considerate of others

> Reliable: Other people can depend on you

> Sincere: Open and genuine

Treating customers as individuals makes them feel appreciated.

- Always use names
- Be **sincere**
- Show body language that conveys sincerity
- Be polite and say "thank you"

{ Building trust is an important part of customer service.

Efficiency: The ability to complete a job with a minimum expenditure of time and effort

Empathy: The capacity to recognize and, to some extent, share, feelings (such as sadness or happiness) experienced by another

Characteristic #4: Address Complaints with Empathy and Efficiency
Addressing complaints with empathy and efficiency will create a positive experience for your customer.

How to handle complaints?

> If something goes wrong you should apologize, even if the customer isn't right
> Deal with problems immediately and ask, "What can I do to make you happy?"
> Ask how you can improve their experience

Often, the customer simply wants to have their complaint heard and receive a heartfelt apology. Complaints give an opportunity for continuous improvement.

TIP: *When addressing complaints, try to see the point of view of the customer. This approach will help you understand the issue and will allow you to be empathetic.*

 Discussion Question

Think of a time you had a complaint and how it was handled.

Did you receive good customer service?

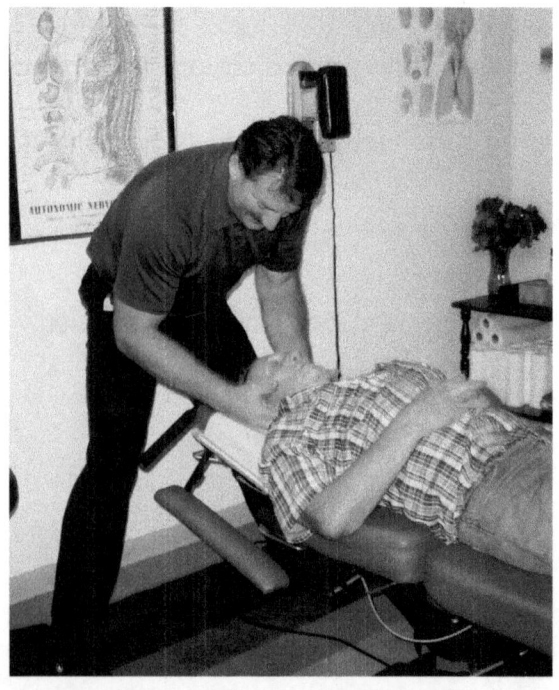

Module 7

 **Practice**

Directions: Write in the correct term from the answer bank to complete each statement.

Answer Bank

Build trust by making promises you can keep

Be present

Address complaints with empathy and efficiency

Be proactive

1. Being helpful, courteous, and knowledgeable describes the following attribute of customer service:

_____

_____

2. Listening with understanding and empathy describes the following attribute of customer service:

_____

_____

3. Asking, "What can I do to make you happy?" is one of the strategies used to support the following attribute of customer service:

_____

_____

4. By identifying and anticipating your customer's needs, you're demonstrating the following attribute of customer service:

_____

_____

 **Assignment**

Directions: Reflecting on your experience with customer service will help you recognize what it takes to have good customer service skills. In the space provided, answer the following questions using complete sentences.

1. Be Present: Write about a time you witnessed someone who was "present" in the workplace. Give an example to support your answer.

2. Be Proactive: Write about a time you witnessed someone who was proactive in the workplace. Give an example to support your answer.

3. Build Trust by Making Promises You Can Keep: Write about a time you witnessed someone perform an action to build trust in the workplace. Give an example to support your answer.

4. Address Complaints with Empathy and Efficiency: Write about a time you witnessed someone address a complaint appropriately. Give an example to support your answer.

5. How can utilizing all of these characteristics ensure good customer service? In your conclusion, describe why these characteristics are important.

_____

_____

_____

_____

_____

_____

_____

_____

_____

_____

_____

Executing Excellence: Be a "Daymaker"

"Daymaker: A person who performs acts of kindness with the intention of making the world a better place."

Customer service is crucial whether you work in an office, a medical clinic, a police station, or any other setting where you interact with the public.

All employees are responsible for quality customer service. You can make an impact just by caring about yourself and those around you. One way to excel in the workplace is to be a "Daymaker." This means practicing Customer Service Characteristics 1-4 (Be Present, Be Proactive, Build Trust by Keeping your Promises, Approach Complaints with Empathy and Efficiency). Try serving with care and compassion. Give 110 percent of yourself all of the time!

"Never doubt that a small group of thoughtful, committed citizens can change the world. Indeed, it's the only thing that ever has."

— Margaret Mead

How to be a Daymaker at Work

Daymaking is not limited to your customers. You can also make the day of a coworker.

> Offer to pick up lunch for someone you know is swamped
> Give someone special a bouquet and have them pass it on to someone else the following day
> Write a thank-you note to the boss
> Acknowledge promotions; send a card to the employee's home
> Offer to drive someone who relies on public transportation
> Pool your money together and buy someone a spa day as a thank you
> Post an employee's baby picture and let everyone guess who it is
> At a monthly meeting, have everyone say something nice about someone else

❓ Discussion Questions

> Can you think of a time someone made your day?
>
> What did he or she do to make you feel special?
>
> How can you pass that feeling on to others?

▶ Practice

Directions: Draw a happy face next to the items that would make someone's day.

Smile at a stranger	
Listen attentively	
Be polite	
Tell someone "you're wrong"	
Pretend to listen	
Do your best to be helpful	
Ignore someone talking to you	
Tell someone they're doing a great job	

Assignment

Directions: Goal setting is a great way to achieve what you set out to do. Imagine yourself as a daymaker. Think about how you can apply the four characteristics of customer service by goal setting. In the space provided below, create a list of goals as directed.

Goals for 30 days	
Goals for first 6 months	
Goals for first year	

Independent Practice 1

Directions: A customer comes into the store where you are working and has a complaint. How would you handle that complaint? Use the answers provided and write the correct response in the appropriate columns.

Ask "What can I do to help?"	Apologize	Ignore the customer	Think about the customer's point of view
Pretend to listen	Problem solve together	Take it personally	Lie to the customer

Handling a Complaint Correctly	Handling a Complaint Incorrectly

Independent Practice 2

Directions: Read the following scenario about Mary, a concierge at a hotel, and Mr. Jones, a new hotel guest checking in. Then answer the following questions.

Scenario

Mary Smith: *Welcome to the Hotel DeLuxe. My name is Mary. How can I help you today?*

Mr. Jones: *Mary, my name is Cliff Jones, and I have a reservation for three nights.*

Mary: *Well, we are delighted to have you here, Mr. Jones! I see you are traveling from Chicago. I hope you had a wonderful trip. Please help yourself to some of our complimentary cookies and fresh brewed coffee while I handle your check-in.*

Mr. Jones: *Thank you, Mary. I'm happy to finally get here; it was a bit of a long trip, and we hit some turbulence mid-flight.*

Mary: *I'm so sorry to hear that. Have you stayed with us before? Are you here for business or for personal reasons?*

Mr. Jones: *No, this is my first visit. Actually, I am here for a job interview.*

Mary: *Oh, how exciting! Well, you have arrived a bit earlier than our normal check-in time, but since you've had such a long, hard trip, let me see if I can get you checked in earlier. After such a difficult trip, you could use some downtime; I know I'd want a nap myself.*

Mr. Jones: *A nap would be wonderful. And I could really use some rest before my dinner interview. If I could have a room away from the parking lot, that would be ideal.*

Mary: *Let me see what I can do, Mr. Jones. (pause) I see here that you've reserved a standard room on the first floor, but the only room that we have at that rate is right next to the parking lot. I'd be happy to offer you an upgrade to a room with a king-sized bed, which is on the second floor, but is on the other side of the property, away from the parking lot. The upgrade would be complimentary. Would that work for you?*

Mr. Jones: *That would be wonderful! And I would be able to check in now?*

Mary: *Absolutely. Please have a seat and feel free to read some of our magazines. I will call a porter to bring your bags to your room, so you don't have to worry about that.*

Mary: *Our restaurant closed 5 minutes ago for the break between lunch and dinner. But, if you would like, I can see if the kitchen can serve you from a limited menu.*

Mr. Jones: *That won't be necessary, but I really appreciate that, Mary. What time does the restaurant open for dinner?*

Mary: *My pleasure, Mr. Jones. Happy hour starts in our lounge at 4 p.m., and registered guests with room keys are invited to enjoy complimentary cocktails and appetizers. You mentioned that you have an appointment tonight, but you may want to take advantage of that on another day. The restaurant opens for dinner at 5 every day. You will be in room 212, but have a seat until the porter arrives. If you need anything during your stay, feel free to call the front desk; my coworkers and I are happy to give you directions or advice on local restaurants or attractions. And thank you for choosing the Hotel DeLuxe for your stay.*

Mr. Jones: *Thank you, Mary! I am looking forward to my stay here.*

1. The hotel concierge showed _____ when hearing about Mr. Jones's long trip.

2. By offering to check with the hotel restaurant, Mary was anticipating the customer's needs by being _____.

3. It was very kind of the hotel concierge to offer a new room to Mr. Jones. She built _____ by offering Mr. Jones a new room and meeting his expectations.

Answer Bank

trust

proactive

empathy

Group Activity

Directions: Complete the folowing tasks.

1. Form a group of 2 to 3 people and read the following scenario.
2. Write answers to the following questions as a group.
3. Create a reference poster that can be displayed at a job site to inform employees about what to do when a situation like this occurs.

Scenario: Medical Office — Disgruntled patient

Patient: *"Excuse me! I have been waiting to see the doctor for 20 minutes! I was here on time, and I should be seen immediately. I am in a lot of pain. What is the hold up? Why are people who came in after me being seen before me? Why should I have to make an appointment if other people take up my time? I am very unhappy. I am going to write a letter of complaint to the office manager and to my insurance company. This is a bunch of nonsense! Where is the nurse?"*

1. If you were the medical worker working at this time, what would you say to this patient?

2. What are some things you could have done to prevent this complaint?

Knowledge Check

Directions: Circle the correct answer.

1. Customer Service is _____.

a.) A series of activities designed to enhance the level of customer satisfaction

b.) The lifeblood of any business

c.) An opportunity to change the perception a customer has of the organization

d.) All of the above

2. Following through on promises you made to customers demonstrates the following characteristic of customer service: _____.

a.) Be present

b.) Be proactive

c.) Build trust by making promises you can keep

d.) Address complaints with empathy and efficiency

3. By identifying and anticipating your customer's needs, you are demonstrating the following characteristic of customer service: _____.

a.) Be present

b.) Be proactive

c.) Build trust by making promises you can keep

d.) Address complaints with empathy and efficiency

4. Asking "What can I do to make you happy?" is one of the strategies used to support the following characteristic of customer service: _____.

a.) Be present

b.) Be proactive

c.) Build trust by making promises you can keep

d.) Address complaints with empathy and efficiency

5. Listening with understanding and empathy describes the following characteristic of customer service: _____.

a.) Be present

b.) Be proactive

c.) Build trust by making promises you can keep

d.) Address complaints with empathy and efficiency

6. According to David Wagner, a Daymaker is:

a.) An individual responsible for delivering quality customer service

b.) A person who performs acts of kindness with the intention of making the world a better place

c.) An efficient person

d.) An individual who cares deeply about their work

7. According to the concept of Daymaking,

a.) You are the only person responsible for delivering quality customer service

b.) Customer service is everyone's responsibility

c.) The company's livelihood depends on customer service

d.) You impact society simply by caring for yourself and everyone in your life

8. Everyone in an organization is responsible for delivering quality customer service.

a.) True

b.) False

9. Which description about customer service is true?

a.) Average customer service is always good enough

b.) Customer service is the responsibility of administration

c.) Customers lost through poor customer service are easy to replace

10. Which is one of the best reasons to provide excellent customer service?

a.) Excellent customer service providers can win prizes, including vacations, from their employers

b.) Work is more personally fulfilling

c.) Companies can hire younger people

d.) There's less work for managers

Module 8

Career Planning

Objectives:

- Develop a plan for the career ahead of you

- Outline your short-term career goals

- Identify the importance of staying current in your field

Career Planning

Define career goals and strategies.

Staying current in your field ensures success.

Career planning is essential for professional success. In this module, you will recognize that having a defined career plan allows you to create the future you desire. We will discuss how to define career goals and strategies to reach your goals. You will also learn the importance of staying current in your field through research and training, ensuring success for your future.

What Do You Already Know?

Directions: Decide if you believe each statement is true (T) or false (F) and write the corresponding letter on the right.

Career Planning	True	False
You should wait until you have a position before you begin to plan for your career.		
After entering your chosen career field, you no longer need to create a career plan.		
Reflecting on what you want to achieve can help you create career goals.		

Why Plan?

Either you've landed your first job, or that's the next milestone in your life. No matter which stage you're in, planning for your career will help pave a secure path for your future.

Creating a plan will help you focus and make strategic decisions to reach your goals. Not only is career planning important to do before you've entered your field, but it's something you should do throughout your professional life. In a career plan, you will:

> Reflect on your needs and wants — Are you looking to make a difference? Support your family? What is your motivation?
> Set career goals — What goals do you need to set in order to succeed in your professional life?
> Determine what you need to do along the way — What do you have to do to continue your career progress?

By actively engaging in developing your career plan, you will give yourself the best chance to fulfill your future goals and be more satisfied with the life you've created.

"Destiny is not a matter of chance; it is a matter of choice. It is not a thing to be waited for; it is a thing to be achieved." — *William Jennings Bryan*

Reflect on Your Future

Take a moment to consider your personal wants and needs. What makes you happy? Do you see yourself someday owning a home? Raising a large family? Traveling the world? Reflecting on your future is important as you develop the steps toward making your vision a reality.

How does your career fit into this picture? In short, what is your ultimate career goal? One excellent way to determine your path to this goal is to work backward.

Long-Term Goal:

> Your Ultimate Career Goal

Mid-path Checkpoint:

> Where do you see yourself in the next 3 to 5 years?
> - What do I have to accomplish at work to reach this point?
> - What additional education and training will I need in order to progress down this path?

Short-Term Action Plan:

> What steps can I take over the next six months to launch my career down the right path?

Short-Term Career Goals

Focus on what you want to achieve. Think about what small steps you can take, as these will become your short-term goals. Short-term career goals are the basis for the plans you make in order to get you close to where you really want to be.

Defining short-term goals

> Can be accomplished starting today, up to six months from now
> Clearly states an **anticipated** achievement
> May include furthering your education, attending training sessions, taking on more responsibilities, etc.

Anticipated: Expected or predicted

Examples include:

> I will visit and learn about all of the services offered through my school's Career Services Office in the next two weeks
> I will revise my résumé within one month
> I will complete my program within four months

"People with clear, written goals, accomplish far more in a shorter period of time than people without them could ever imagine."

— Brian Tracy

 **Assignment**

Directions: In the space provided below, write down four short-term goals that will help you reach your career destination.

1.

2.

3.

4.

Practice

Directions: Circle the appropriate goals for beginning a career.

I will write a cover letter within two weeks.	I will just let a job fall into place.	I will complete an externship within four months.
I will complete my degree within six months.	I will attend a training session within two months.	I will land a management position as my first job.

Strategies for Reaching Your Goals

Working toward your goals is a challenge! Once you've defined your goals, develop strategies to help you reach them.

Try these strategies:

> Identify specific skills required for your intended job
  – Determine the specific training or education required and plan for how you will complete it.
  – Pursue any additional skills that would help you to become more proficient in your chosen field.

> Advertise your goals
  – Share your goals with family and friends, instructors, and supervisors. You never know who might be willing and able to help you reach your goals.

> Network for opportunities
  – Find ways to network with others at school, work, and in your community.
  – Volunteer for projects that will enable you to develop and cultivate your professional network.
  – Seek out people who can serve as **mentors** — ask them for help and thank them when they provide you with advice and guidance.

Mentor: A person who advises or trains

Discussion Question

Which of these strategies can you implement to reach your specific goals?

Develop a Career Plan

Similar to a blueprint when building a home, a career plan is the blueprint for building your professional career. It is comprised of your goals and the identified strategies to reach those goals. Writing this plan down will bring these goals to life. You will be able to recognize the steps you need to take in order to reach these goals, which will become action steps.

Action steps:

> Answer "how" you will reach your goals
> Break down goals into smaller milestones or steps
> Include concrete target dates to keep you on task

After writing down your action steps, you will need to take action and complete those tasks.

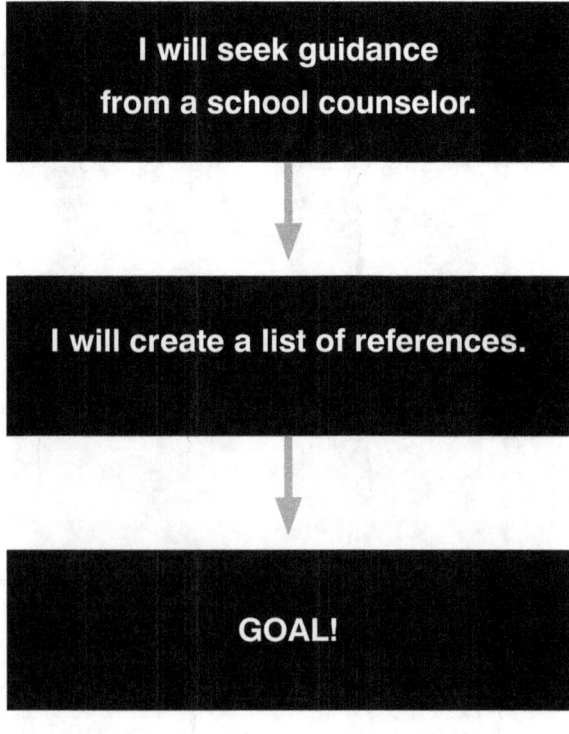

Assignment

Directions: Begin your career plan by completing the table below.

1. Goal Write one of your short-term goals.	
2. Requirements What will it take to reach this goal? Add skills, trainings, education, etc.	
3. Current Skills Write down any current skills related to your goal.	
4. Plan What are the exact steps you plan to take in order to achieve your goal?	

Planning and Preparation — Training and Experience

There are additional items and experiences you can use to help plan and prepare for your career. Learning more about your field outside of the classroom should be at the top of the list.

Learn by doing — gain experience by seeking out opportunities for hands-on learning through:

> Volunteering
> An externship
> Student organizations
> Professional and trade organizations
> Part-time work

You will be able to practice your skills, make connections with people in your field, and, most importantly, have the ability to make clear academic and professional decisions.

TIP: *Use the Internet or your school's Career Services Department to find opportunities for hands-on experiences.*

Planning and Preparation — Staying Current in Your Field

As the world, and specifically technology, continues to change, so will elements of your career. Try to stay up-to-date on the latest trends and advancements. Research and seek out more information by joining groups, signing up for newsletters, and regularly reading industry updates found on the Internet or other publications.

Field Requirements

Anticipate further **certifications** or **licenses** you will need. You may need to take an extra course, earn a new certificate, or update certificates you already have. No matter the situation, take ownership of your career and make sure you are keeping all certifications up-to-date.

Planning ahead for these requirements allows you to complete important refresher courses or training in a timely manner. It all becomes part of the plan, preparing you for the future you've desired.

> Certifications: Meeting eligibility requirements, such as education or experience

> Licenses: A permit to perform a specific skill, carry on a trade, etc.

 **Assignment**

Directions: Use the Internet to research the field you are entering. Write down any requirements you will need to complete.

Note: If Internet access is not available, this can be done at home or at a library.

_____

_____

_____

_____

_____

Module 8

Your Career Path

Reflecting on the life you'd like to have 10, 15, or 20 years from now is a good way to keep your professional life in perspective. The choices you make now will directly effect your future. Make the right decisions to get where you want to be. Plan and prepare yourself for the life ahead of you.

Your career plan is a **living document**.

> Living document: A document that is continually edited or updated

> Write down your career plan and keep it in a convenient location
> Reflect on it often — check off completed tasks and add new ones
> Change it as you change in your career

You owe it to yourself to achieve professional success. Remain focused and continue to set goals to keep on a successful career path.

"As for the future, your task is not to foresee it, but to enable it." — *Antoine de Saint-Exupéry*

Independent Practice 1

Directions: Decide which of the following advice is good advice — a "Do" — or bad advice — a "Don't." Write the advice in the appropriate column.

Try to gain hands-on experience	Reach out to your school's career services	Take time to reflect on your professional future
Expect a job to just happen	Give up on your goals	Wait until you've received a job to create goals

Good Professional Advice "Do"	Bad Professional Advice "Don't"

Module 8

Independent Practice 2

Directions: Read the scenario below and complete the table by writing in the action steps Steven should take. Then, develop two additional steps on your own.

Scenario
Steven is a student in a pharmacist technician program. As he works on his career plan, think about the action steps he should take to reach this goal and complete the activity that follows.

| Visit a few facilitites | Perform mediocre in class | Complete five applications | Meet with a counselor in a career center | Research externship opportunities |

What action steps should Steven complete to reach his career goal of landing a job within a month of completing his program?

Group Activity

Directions: As a group, read the following scenario and use the questions below to guide the group in coming up with a career plan for Brianna.

Scenario: *Brianna is in the last semester of her senior year in high school. She does not like school that much, and wants to drop out. However, she wants a career as a medical assistant. Brianna has a part-time job that she needs to keep. How can Brianna reach her goal of becoming a medical assistant?*

Think about the following:

> What are her short-term goals?
> What is a good short-term action plan?
> What strategies can she use for reaching these goals?

Brianna's Career Plan

Brianna's Long-Term Goal	
1.	

Brianna's Short-Term Goal	
1.	2.

Action Steps to Reach Her Short-Term Goals	
1.	2.
3.	4.

Advice for Brianna (find mentors, work on certificates, etc.)	
1.	2.
3.	4.

Knowledge Check

Directions: Circle the correct answer.

1. Short-term career goals usually occur in the span of

a.) Two years

b.) Up to six months

c.) Up to two weeks

d.) One year

2. Developing a career plan will help you

a.) Identify the steps you need to take to reach your goals

b.) Define your career goals

c.) Have a say in your future

d.) All of the above

3. It is important to have concrete steps and target dates when developing action steps.

a.) True

b.) False

4. Some of the strategies to help you reach your goals include

a.) Identifying specific skills you require

b.) Advertising your goals

c.) Networking for opportunities

d.) All of the above

5. Even after completing your education, there is a good chance you will need to renew your certifications throughout your career.

a.) True

b.) False

6. In all fields it is important to stay current and knowledgeable of any changes or advancements.

a.) True

b.) False

7. In a career plan, action steps help to

a.) Determine how you will reach your goals

b.) Keep you focused

c.) Break down goals into smaller milestones or steps

d.) All of the above

8. The secret to a successful career includes

a.) Staying up-to-date in your field

b.) Creating a goal oriented career plan

c.) Reflecting on your plan and making changes if necessary

d.) All of the above

9. You should wait until you have a position before you begin planning for your career.

a.) True

b.) False

10. It is a good idea to learn more about your field outside of the classroom, because you will

a.) Gain a better perspective on the field you are entering

b.) Be able to make clearer academic and professional decisions

c.) Make connections with people in your field

d.) All of the above

Module 9

Business Basics

Objectives:

– Describe the elements of a successful business operation

– Analyze the value of people, processes, and technology in business

– Identify the essential functions of a business

Business Basics

Turn a great idea or a great product into a thriving enterprise.

Learn the fundamental elements that apply to every business.

In this module, you will learn the fundamental elements that apply to every business from small companies to large corporations. You will see how these elements apply to any successful business by following the story of Kai, who is starting Kai's Cookie Company. This fictional business mirrors the stories of so many people who have a burning desire to turn a great idea or a great product into a thriving enterprise.

What Do You Already Know?

Directions: These services are offered in a neighborhood next to a college campus. Place an X next to each company/service you think will be successful.

Company/Service:

____ Pizza delivery service   ____ Mortgage company   ____ Pet store

____ Cell phone store   ____ Coffee shop

Five Questions Every Business Must Answer

When launching a new business, there are several questions that must be considered:

1. Do I have a business that's capable of working successfully?
2. Are there enough people or organizations interested in my product or service?
3. Is my **business structure** appropriate for my operation?
4. Can I manage the essential functional areas of this business?
5. Can I make a profit?

> **Business structure:** Type of legal organization for the company

Many details need to be considered in order for a business to function successfully. Throughout this module, you will be guided through the journey of Kai, who is starting his business, Kai's Cookie Company. The cookie image shows you how Kai's business relates to the lesson.

Kai's Cookie Company

1. *How will Kai's Cookie Company distinguish itself from the competition?*
2. *Who will be Kai's customers? How will he market his cookies?*
3. *Should Kai be a sole proprietor, LLC, or corporation?*
4. *Can Kai manage the responsibilities involved in the leadership, marketing and sales, finance, operations, and administration of running a company?*
5. *How can Kai balance his creative vision with the realities of the financial issues involved in running a business?*

The Foundation of a Business

Whether you plan to start your own business or join an existing one, it is important to examine the foundation of the business. A successful business must have the following four components:

> Value: How much something is worth

> Consumers: People who purchase goods or services

> Demand — there is a want, need, or problem
> Supply — a product, service, or solution to meet that demand
> Reasonably priced goods — the ability to recognize the value of a product/service and determine a reasonable price that appeals to consumers
> Profitability — the ability to make money

Foundation for Kai's Cookie Company

Kai asked himself:

Does anyone have the want/need for delicious cookies?

Yes, desserts have a consistent demand.

Does my product (cookies) satisfy the demand?

Yes, neighbors and friends rave about my cookies and have offered to buy them.

Is it affordable?

I researched cookie prices of competitors, taking into account the size of the cookies, the cost of ingredients, and labor. I can charge between $1 and $1.75 per cookie.

Am I making a profit?

I will charge $1.50 for each cookie. My friends told me that it is a fair price and I'm confident I can make a profit if I sell as many as I plan to.

 Practice

---

Directions: Imagine a business that you want to create. Think of two additional questions that you'd like to research to learn more about your ideal customers.

1. Are your customers male or female?

2. How old are they?

3. How will your product or service help them?

4. _____

5. _____

Module 9

Types of Business

There are several types of business structures defined in the legal system. Legal and tax issues need to be considered when choosing a business structure.

Review these common business structures:

> **Shareholder:** An owner of shares in a company

Sole Proprietor	Business owned by an individual
	Great for independent contractors, retail, and service businesses
Corporation	Business owned by **shareholders**
	Can be public — shares sold on the stock exchange
	Can be private — shares not available to the general public
	Provides legal and financial protection for shareholders
Limited Liability Company (LLC)	Ownership typically by two or more people
	Blends elements of partnerships and corporate structures
Nonprofit	Money earned from operations must be reinvested into the business
	Does not pay federal or state taxes
	Universities, churches, and charities are often formed as nonprofits

Kai's Business Structure

Since Kai is starting his own company, he has decided to set up his business as a sole proprietor. He is the only person who owns the business and will retain any profits or losses. Kai needs to remember to set aside money during the year so he can pay the appropriate taxes during tax season.

What Do You Need to Run a Business?

Even if you don't plan to run your own business, understanding how a business operates will provide you with a valuable perspective. It takes people, processes, and technology to run a business.

People	People are resources that contribute labor and skills to the business
Processes	Processes provide a consistent way of organizing activities to complete tasks
Technology	Technology aids a company in efficiency, communication, quality, and documentation

Running Kai's Business

Kai asked a lot of successful business people, "What does it take?"

People: *Kai was told not to try to do everything himself, but rather get a solid team in place. Kai should focus on creating the vision and defining the goals. The people he hires to help must be knowledgeable and willing to work and contribute.*

Processes: *Kai was advised to modify his process and method of organizing his tasks, to build in structured time to discuss and revise new ideas.*

Technology: *It was suggested to Kai to use a computer system and accounting software to track and manage the finances of the company.*

Practice

Directions: Complete each statement by writing in the correct term.

1. People who are willing to make a purchase have a _____ that is unmet or must be fulfilled.

2. The _____ must adequately satisfy the demand.

3. In order for a sale to be completed, the product or service must be _____ and provide value.

Answer Bank
supply
reasonably priced
need
profit

4. If you wish to stay in business, you must learn how to maintain a _____.

Essential Functions for Running a Business

Running a business requires organization, planning, and processes. Business functions are processes put in place to support the mission of a business. Each function has its own role in order to help the business run efficiently.

Five essential functions that must be addressed in a business:

1. Leadership	2. Marketing and Sales	3. Financial	4. Operations	5. Administration

Kai's Functions

Kai sat down and brainstormed the essential functions for his business. He realized his business needed strong leadership, excellent marketing and sales, individuals to handle the operations (baking cookies!), and administration. He focused on each one, identifying the roles of those functions.

Essential Function #1: Leadership

The most important function of any business is leadership. The other areas are essential, but without solid leadership a business will fail!

Leadership **derives** from the leaders in the organization working toward a common goal. A great way to strengthen leadership is to **publicize** the purpose of the company through a mission statement.

A mission statement is constructed from the vision, values, and goals of the organization. To create a mission statement, you need to identify:

> The vision—what the company would like to share with the world
> The values—what's important to the organization and the people in it
> The goals—what the company plans to accomplish

Derive: To obtain from something

Publicize: To make something widely known

TIP: *Use the internet to research mission statements.*

Leadership in Kai's Cookie Company

The vision: *Kai would like to sell delicious cookies to everyone.*

The values: *Kai believes that food products should be handmade using quality ingredients.*

The goals: *Kai would like to earn a living doing what he loves, which is making cookies.*

Mission Statement: *The mission of Kai's Cookie Company is to provide homemade cookies baked with quality ingredients to customers.*

 **Assignment**

Directions: Using the knowledge from this lesson, write a mission statement for a fictional business. Remember to include the vision, values, and goals.

Mission Statement:

_____

_____

_____

_____

_____

_____

_____

Essential Function #2: Marketing and Sales

Businesses need marketing and sales to make customers aware of the product or service available to them.

Marketing: Letting people know about your product or service
Sales: Selling the product or service to a customer

Marketing and sales provides answers to the following:

> Is our advertising reaching our potential consumers and does it reflect our mission?

> Do we correctly identify the value of our product and an appropriate price?

> Do we listen and respond to our customers?

> Do we accurately estimate our sales projections and produce accordingly?

Kai's Marketing and Sales

Kai's sales team created an informational brochure that can be handed out to local businesses interested in purchasing their cookies. In an effort to advertise the company, Kai created a Facebook business account. On the site, customers can suggest new cookie flavors and provide feedback on current products.

Assignment

Directions: Create a fictional company and market your business. Construct a flyer to help sell your product or service, and incorporate as many details as you can from this lesson.

Essential Function #3: Financial

The financial aspect of business involves tracking revenues, controlling expenses, and making decisions about how money will be used for future spending. Important business decisions are made based on the financial reporting function of a business.

Accounting: The tracking and controlling of a business's finances

> Maintains accurate financial and accounting statements
> Tracks **receivables and payables**
> Creates a system to meet legal requirements

Receivables and payables: Money that is owed to the business and money the business owes to others

Financial Management: The decision-making of a business's finances

> Manages the amount of money coming in and out of the business
> Ensures purchase decisions are wise
> Determines a realistic value of the business

TIP: *Don't hesitate to seek the help of financial professionals, such as accountants and financial managers.*

Kai's Financial Function

Kai purchased software to help with financial management. By organizing his finances, he is able to analyze sales, expenses, and cash flow issues that impact daily operations. Because this is all new to Kai, he needed to find some outside help with financial management. Kai hired an accountant to help with taxes and other accounting issues.

Essential Function #4: Operations

Business operations are the ongoing activities involved in running a business. These operational questions should be asked and revisited on a regular basis:

Acquire: To buy or obtain

Raw materials: The basic materials from which a product is made

> How do we **acquire** the best **raw materials** at the best price? (For a products company.)
> What are the most efficient manufacturing processes for our product?
> Can we meet the demand of the customers?
> How can we consistently ensure timely delivery?
> Are we managing our talent and resources effectively?

Kai's Operations

Kai researched wholesale companies that sell flour, sugar, and other ingredients vital to his product. He found a local, organic supplier for his raw ingredients. In addition to securing a quality supplier, Kai added value to his cookies by using exclusively organic ingredients.

Essential Function #5: Administration

Administration is essential to meet the business standards and rules and regulations in today's business world.

What are the major administrative functions and how does each contribute to the success of the business?

Human Resources	Legal	Information Systems and Networks
Employee record management	Business contracts	Data storage
Employee hiring and training	Risk management (insurance)	Data access, reliability, and security
Compliance with wage and hour regulations	Business meets regulations	Filing and document management

TIP: *Well-drafted contracts can save money and decrease liability for businesses.*

Kai's Administration

Kai hired an individual to administer the human resources of his cookie company. He also found a small business lawyer to help with contracts on an as-needed basis.

He then hired an outside company to set up a computer system.

Summary

Kai's Cookie Company, like any business, will need the proper mix of people, processes, and technology to be successful. A shared vision and passion among team members, effective business processes, and the right technology will help this business thrive.

As you are growing professionally, keep in mind the essentials of running a business and use that information to your advantage as you progress through your own career!

"Disneyland is the work of love. We didn't go into Disneyland with just the idea of making money." — *Walt Disney*

Kai's Cookie Company

Even with all the people Kai was able to hire, he still has to work very hard, every day. This type of work is what Kai enjoys, and he is able to take pride in it. He feels fulfilled professionally and wouldn't want to do anything else. Yummm!

Independent Practice 1

Directions: Read the following scenario, and then circle the essential functions of a business that Kai needs to get started.

Essential Functions

Administration
Demand
Financial
Operations
Consumers
Leadership
Profit
Marketing and Sales

Scenario

Kai: *I am so excited! I know I have a great product that people will buy, and I will finally have a chance to make my vision come true.*

Friend: *That's great, Kai, your cookies ARE good, but how do you plan to make your business successful?*

Kai: *You know, I need to be smart about this so I can improve my chances. I know there is a demand for my product, and that I can make a profit. I need to start planning the functions for my business.*

Independent Practice 2

Directions: Draw a line to match each term with the correct definition.

Demand	Marketing	Profitability	Accounting	Human Resources

The ability to make a profit	Manages employees and ensures compliance with wage/hours	Getting the message to those people who can buy	A want or need	The tracking and controlling of finances

Module 9

Group Activity

Directions: Form a group. Choose a business from the list below.

> Mr. Pickles' Pickles
> Walter's Walkers — Professional Dog Walking Service
> Sue's Sandwich Shop

How would you get started to successfully run this business? Work with your group to explain what you would do. Use eight of the thirteen vocabulary words from this module to write a paragaph about running your business.

Vocabulary

Acquire	Raw materials
Business structure	Value
Consumers	Shareholders
Perspective	Advertising
Sales projections	Derive
Publicize	Receivables and payables
Thrive	

Example: I will <u>advertise</u> Walter's Walkers — Professional Dog Walking Service, at the local pet store, so my potential <u>consumers</u> will know about the <u>value</u> my business offers.

_____

_____

_____

_____

_____

_____

_____

Knowledge Check

Directions: Circle the correct answer.

1. In order for a business to be successful, you must have the following:

a.) A demand for a product or service

b.) A human resources specialist

c.) Overpriced goods

d.) State-of-the-art technology

2. As a sole proprietor, you must be able to do everything yourself.

a.) True

b.) False

3. What element(s) are valuable in creating a successful business?

a.) People

b.) Processes

c.) Technology

d.) All of the above

4. The product or service must adequately satisfy the _____.

a.) Demand

b.) Profit

c.) Technology

d.) Process

5. What is an important part of creating a mission statement?

a.) People

b.) Values

c.) Technology

d.) Supply/demand

6. Marketing is _____

a.) Making sure customers can make a purchase

b.) Getting the message to those people who have the ability to purchase your product

c.) The ability to make a sufficient profit

d.) Financial management of the business

7. The financial function of a business includes accounting and financial decision-making.

a.) True

b.) False

8. Business operations seek to

a.) Produce the product or service in the most cost efficient and quality manner

b.) Ensure purchase decisions are wise

c.) Manage revenues and costs to optimize taxes

d.) Make sure the advertising is reaching the right markets

9. Administrative function(s) every business needs to consider are

a.) Human resources

b.) Legal

c.) Information systems and networks

d.) All of the above

10. A Limited Liability Company blends elements of partnerships and corporate structures.

a.) True

b.) False

Externship Excellence

Objectives:

– Describe the purpose of an externship and what you will gain

– Discuss how to prepare for your externship

– Distinguish why an externship is an opportunity of a lifetime

Externship Excellence

Gaining a better understanding of a career.

Take advantage of the experience.

A chance to truly get a glimpse into the career ahead of you: An Externship. Externships are a great opportunity for students to practice skills, make connections in the field, and ultimately have a better understanding of thecareer. In this module, you will learn about externships, what to expect, how to prepare and take advantage of the experience, and why an externship is truly an experience of a lifetime.

What Do You Already Know?

Directions: Choose if each statement is true or false and place a check mark in the appropriate box.

	True	False
An externship is a hands-on opportunity to work in your field		
A school's Career Services office is a great resource to help students learn more about externships		
Externships provide a chance to make connections		

What is an Externship?

At or near the conclusion of students' coursework, many college programs have an externship requirement. During an externship, students gain work experience in their field of study. This opportunity enables students to demonstrate and reinforce the knowledge and skills presented and practiced throughout their training program.

Most of us have grand dreams of the ideal job. But what do we really know about what it would be like to work on that job every day? What would the working environment be like? What skills would it take to really do the job?

One way to find out is through your externship while you are in school and preparing for your career. So, what more do you need to know about an externship?

TIP: Ask someone who's completed an externship about their experience.

> Sponsor: A trusted counselor, guide, or tutor at the externship site

Describing the Basics

An externship program is designed to expose students to various careers so they are better able to make wise career decisions. The purpose of the program is purely educational, and the **sponsors** invest significant effort into designing experiences for externs.

Overview

> Shadow: Follow the professional and observe daily work

- Most externships are typically short-term, and students complete a required number of hours
- Students **shadow** an employee at a sponsoring organization
- Depending on the school, externs may or may not receive college credit for their time
- Externs do not generally perform for the employers, but may perform small office tasks or assist with projects, and learn the environment of the field
- Externs are typically not compensated for time spent at the sponsoring company

 Assignment

Directions: Open a web browser and use a search engine to complete the following steps.

Step 1: Connect to your school's website.
Step 2: Search the site for information about externships in your field.
Step 3: Answer the following questions in the space provided.

- Is there contact information for someone who can help you find out more about externships? Describe what you find.
- Are externships required in your program?
- Is there any feedback from people who have completed externships?

_____

_____

_____

_____

_____

_____

_____

_____

What's in it for Me?

An externship is a major part of your career experience, but do you know the benefits and how you can make the most of the experience? As long as you know what's in it for you, focus on what you can do to make the most of an externship.

Learn what you can expect to gain from an externship.

A Glimpse into the Career Ahead of You	Build a Résumé or Portfolio	Improve Your Own Skill Set	Network and Showcase Your Talents
An externship provides an opportunity for you to understand the career you are entering. You will shadow employees, and in the process will gain a perspective on your career choice.	Document the skills and the experience you achieve during your externship. List these accomplishments on your résumé and build your portfolio.	Recognizing learned concepts in the workplace reinforces your knowledge and improves your skills. Make observations and seek out opportunities to perform tasks under the guidance of a skilled employee.	Ask questions and make relationships with people in the company. If given the opportunity, demonstrate your talents and show the team what you can do.

Discussion Questions

What do I expect to gain from my externship experience?

What do I anticipate being my biggest takeaway?

How an Externship Works

Treat your externship like it's an audition for a big part in a stage production or a long job interview. Know the expectations required by both your school and externship site, and prepare yourself to exceed everyone's expectations.

You will either need to apply for an externship or you will receive a placement through your school. In both cases, the best way to learn about your school's externship program is to visit the Career Services office.

The Career Services office provides students and alumni with opportunities to define, develop, and realize their potential. Visit your school's Career Services office to:

> Find out how placements work and what you need to do
> Gain assistance in preparing your résumé
> Learn useful tools and resources to get you on the right path

TIP: *To learn about your program's externship requirements, review your school's catalog or search on your school's website. The school catalog contains the location and hours of operation for your school's Career Services office.*

"It doesn't matter how many resources you have — if you don't know how to use them, they will never be enough." — *Albert Einstein*

 **Practice**

Directions: Determine if the statement is true or false and place a check mark in the correct column.

Statement about Externships	True	False
Externships can sometimes be a graduation requirement		
All schools arrange externships for students		
You will gain experience from an externship		
You will be paid for your externship work		
You can come and go on your own schedule		
You will make connections with new people		

What to Expect During Your Externship

Prepare for your externship by anticipating the tasks ahead of you and identifying what you plan to achieve.

During your externship, you can expect to:

> Make observations
> Ask questions
> Attend meetings
> Conduct informational interviews with professionals
> Work directly with customers or clients
> Get career guidance
> Practice skills
> Tour the facilities

Evaluate your personal goals and create objectives for your externship by asking yourself these questions:

> What are my personal career goals?
> What benefits do I hope to achieve?
> What kind of impression do I want to make?

 **Assignment**

Directions: Think about your personal career goals, what you want to achieve, and the impression you want to make. In the space below, write three objectives for your externship experience.

Example Objective: *I will conduct two informational interviews by the end of my externship.*

Objective 1:

Objective 2:

Objective 3:

Getting Started with Your Externship

Before you begin your externship, ask yourself, "What's the best way to be prepared?"

Get started with your externship by completing this checklist:

> Call the organization and confirm the address, start time, and where you will meet when you arrive.
> Find out if you need to bring a lunch and prepare a lunch if necessary.
> Prepare your work clothing by making sure it is clean and wrinkle-free.
> Pack a résumé and any **additional documents** requested by the sponsoring company.
> Plan how you will travel to the externship location. Conduct a trial run so you know how to get there and how much time it will take.
> Research the organization you are assigned to work with.

Additional documents: You may need to bring forms from the school or proof of certain immunizations

Use the externship to your advantage. Prepare and make the most of your experience. Remember that your externship becomes a priority at this moment and is a foundation for a successful career.

TIP: *Research the externship's company website and learn about the leaders of the company.*

Make a Great Impression

Remind yourself that your externship is like an audition, so it's crucial to make a great impression. Think about what you can do to impress and perform at your externship site.

In addition to following your **school's conduct policies**, follow these guidelines to make a lasting impression:

> School conduct policy: A set of principles and expectations for all students

- > Show up on time or early to your externship site every day and complete shift hours
- > Dress in required work clothing, and be clean and neatly groomed
- > Ask questions and meet the people in the organization
- > When appropriate, discuss your talents
- > Bring a pen and notepad and take notes
- > Communicate clearly, be respectful, and use good manners
- > Make an effort to create relationships and build your **professional network**
- > Be present by showing you're interested, listen **attentively**, and get involved

> Professional network: A support system of sharing information and services among individuals

> Attentive: Giving care or attentionals

 Discussion Question

What can I do during my externship to make sure I leave a positive lasting impression?

Practice

Directions: Determine how you can make the best impression during your externship and make it a successful experience. Write 3 things you can do to make the best impression in the spaces provided below.

Show up on time or early	Talk and text on your cell phone	Show off by trying to do everything
Be uninterested	Treat the externship like a job interview	Dress in appropriate clothing

1. _____

2. _____

3. _____

Build Relationships to Create Future Opportunities

Through an externship, you will meet many individuals in your career field. In most cases you will be directed to shadow a sponsor or mentor. Make an effort to build a relationship with your sponsor and anyone else you meet during your externship. It would also be a good idea to gather contact information for individuals you meet.

You never know when the connections you make as an extern might come in handy. This experience could lead to possible job opportunities either within that organization or a partnering one.

TIP: *If you haven't already, create a LinkedIn account. Add individuals you meet during your externship to stay connected.*

"The art and science of asking questions is the source of all knowledge." — *Thomas Berger*

What to Do After Finishing an Externship

You wouldn't run a race, get to the finish line, and walk right past it, right? The same idea is relevant for an externship. Although you may be on your last shift, there are a few tasks that must be completed to bring your experience to a close. Make sure to take the time to properly finish your externship.

> Follow up with the employer and school upon completion of the externship
> Thank your sponsor and let them know what you've learned
> Update your résumé upon completion of the externship
> Post your experiences on your LinkedIn profile
> Request recommendations, if appropriate (these can either be posted to your LinkedIn account or be typed letters, written by the employer or the school faculty member reviewing your assignments if it is for credit, or both)
> Make sure all course credit–related assignments are completed and submitted on time

Make the Most of Your Externship

Remember that your externship provides an opportunity for possible future employment. Make the most of your experience through preparation, planning, and creating expectations for yourself. Leave the people you meet with a lasting impression.

Summary

An externship is much more than a graduation requirement. Use your externship as a chance to practice skills, make a great impression with a potential future employer, and add value to your résumé. Ask the right questions, show genuine interest, and keep yourself busy. Your externship may just be the experience you need to get the job you want!

"Action is the most foundational key to success." — *Pablo Picasso*

Independent Practice 1

Directions: Read the scenario and determine what Seth forgot to do to prepare for his externship.

Scenario

Seth is starting his externship tomorrow and wants to make sure he accomplished everything on his to-do list. He already packed his lunch, which was in the refrigerator. He decided to double-check the start time of the shift to make sure he would be there on time. Next, Seth packed a notepad along with a few pencils to take notes and gather contact information.

Thinking he was all packed, Seth felt it was a good idea to get mentally prepared for the externship. He sat down and thought about the skills he learned in school, what his goals were, and some questions he wanted to ask. He wrote down a few questions on a piece of paper and placed it in his backpack. He would make sure to ask those questions when given an opportunity tomorrow.

Seth went to sleep excited for the day ahead.

Write the things Seth forgot to do in the space below.

Pack a résumé	Pack books to read at the externship	Print out directions
Make sure clothing is clean and ready	Stay up late the night before	Bring iPod to listen to music

_____
_____
_____
_____
_____

Independent Practice 2

Directions: In this module you learned that externships are a valuable experience. From the list below, choose five beneficial outcomes you plan to gain from your own externship. Rank them in order of their importance to you.

> To add value to your résumé
> To earn college credit
> To develop your professional network
> To meet new friends
> To practice your skills
> To make some extra cash
> To gain experience in a career field
> To learn more about a career field of your choice

1.

2.

3.

4.

5.

 **Group Activity**

Directions: Review the first page of this module to gain a better understanding of what you can gain from an externship. Create a poster with your group, describing the benefits of an externship and share with the class. Include pictures or drawings that relate to your poster.

Example:

IMPROVE MY SKILL SET

Observe others doing the work I want to do

Get guidance from a skilled employee

Learn about behaviors and tasks I will need to use

Recognize concepts that I have learned

Reinforce my knowledge

Get comfortable in the new environment

Knowledge Check

Directions: Circle the correct answer.

1. An externship is a learning opportunity that provides students with a chance to work in the field they are studying.

a.) True

b.) False

2. The purpose of an externship is for students to

a.) Make connections with individuals in the field

b.) Practice skills learned in school

c.) Gain perspective on what it would be like to work in the career field

d.) All of the above

3. Externships offer an exciting chance to

a.) Earn extra money

b.) Meet new friends

c.) Expand your classroom studies with real-world experience

d.) None of the above

4. A school's Career Services Office can provide students with information about externships.

a.) True

b.) False

5. During an externship, students will most likely be

a.) Making observations

b.) Interviewing employees

c.) Attending meetings

d.) All of the above

6. Students participating in an externship will shadow an employee.

a.) True

b.) False

7. You will have a successful externship experience if you

a.) Make an effort to build relationships

b.) Show you're interested, listen attentively, and get involved

c.) Communicate clearly, be respectful, and use good manners

d.) All of the above

8. During an externship, students are expected to
a.) Travel to the externship, no matter the distance
b.) Arrive on time and complete shift hours
c.) Be engaged in the employer's environment
d.) All of the above

9. The people you meet during your externship can become part of your
a.) Friend circle
b.) Family
c.) Network
d.) None of the above

10. An externship can improve a foundation for successful employment.
a.) True
b.) False

www.ingramcontent.com/pod-product-compliance
Lightning Source LLC
Chambersburg PA
CBHW060344010526
44117CB00017B/2959